# PLOTTING AND WRITING
## SUSPENSE FICTION

## Books by Patricia Highsmith

STRANGERS ON A TRAIN

THE GLASS CELL

THE TWO FACES OF JANUARY

THE CRY OF THE OWL

THIS SWEET SICKNESS

A GAME FOR THE LIVING

DEEP WATER

THE TALENTED MR. RIPLEY

THE BLUNDERER

THE STORY-TELLER

THOSE WHO WALK AWAY

THE TREMOR OF FORGERY

RIPLEY UNDER GROUND

A DOG'S RANSOM

### SHORT STORIES

THE SNAIL-WATCHER AND OTHER STORIES

# Plotting

# and Writing

# Suspense Fiction

by PATRICIA HIGHSMITH

The Writer, Inc. / BOSTON / PUBLISHERS

Library of Congress Catalog Card Number: 66-11138

ISBN: 0-87116-072-2

Printed in the United States of America

# CONTENTS

Chapter                                                         Page

PREFACE TO THE NEW EDITION                        vii
I     THE GERM OF AN IDEA                                  1
II    MAINLY ON USING EXPERIENCES                    11
III   THE SUSPENSE SHORT STORY                        23
IV    DEVELOPMENT                                          33
V     PLOTTING                                               48
VI    THE FIRST DRAFT                                       56
VII   THE SNAGS                                              76
VIII  THE SECOND DRAFT                                    91
IX    THE REVISIONS                                         96
X     THE CASE HISTORY OF A NOVEL: *The Glass
         Cell*                                               102
XI    THE BOOK                                              125
XII   SOME NOTES ON SUSPENSE IN GENERAL          140

# Preface to the New Edition

In this preface to the second edition of Plotting and Writing Suspense Fiction, I would first like to saw how glad I am that the first edition brought so many letters from people young, middle-aged, even a few old. This book is meant for people of any age who want to write fiction, and to such people I give credit already for being writers, because they intend, for better or for worse, to bare their hearts, their personalities, their personal quirks to the public gaze.

I have dwelt as much on my failures as my successes here, because one can learn a lot from failures. By describing my sometimes formidable losses of time and effort, perhaps I can save other writers from going through the same things.

But I didn't speak of luck. I had luck, undeniably, even though I don't believe in luck. Maybe much of luck is due to the right publicity at the right time, and that I do discuss in this book.

Since the first edition of Plotting and Writing, I have written four books and had a book of short stories published. One of the books, *Those Who Walk Away,* was bought by Columbia Pictures. Tom Ripley has made a second appearance in *Ripley under Ground,*

and he again goes free at the end—unlike the film
*Purple Noon,* made from the first Ripley novel, in which
(in the film) he is trapped at the end. And that film is
only ten years old now. They say censorship is loosening
up, that there isn't any. Let's hope it touches the crime-
in-fiction as well as the sex scene. As to recent achieve-
ments, however, I am proudest of a comment in the
London *Times Literary Supplement* of last month: "She
is the crime writer who comes closest to giving crime
writing a good name."

Many beginning writers think that established writers
must have a secret formula for success. Above all, this
book dispels that idea. There is no secret of success in
writing except individuality, or call it personality. And
since every person is different, it is only for the individual
to express his difference from the next fellow. This is
what I call the opening of the spirit. But it isn't mystic.
It is merely a kind of freedom—freedom organized.

So this isn't a textbook, or a how-to-do-it book. It will
not make anybody work harder. But it will, I hope, make
people who want to write realize what is already within
them.

PATRICIA HIGHSMITH

# PLOTTING AND WRITING
## SUSPENSE FICTION

CHAPTER 1

## ✺ THE GERM OF AN IDEA

THE first person you should think of pleasing, in writing a book, is yourself. If you can amuse yourself for the length of time it takes to write a book, the publishers and the readers can and will come later.

Every story with a beginning, middle, and end has suspense; a suspense story presumably has it more so. In this book I shall use the word *suspense* in the way the book trade uses it, as meaning stories with a threat of violent physical action and danger, or the danger and action itself. Another characteristic of the suspense story is that it provides entertainment in a lively and usually superficial sense. One does not expect profound thought or long sections without action in a suspense story. But the beauty of the suspense genre is that a writer can write profound thoughts and have some sections without physical action if he wishes to, because the framework is an essentially lively story. *Crime and Punishment* is a splendid example of this. In fact, I think most of Dostoyevsky's books would be called suspense books, were they being published today for the first time. But he would be asked to cut, because of production costs.

### Developing story germs

What is the germ of an idea? It is probably all things to all writers: A child falling on a sidewalk and spilling his ice cream cone. A respectable-looking man in a grocer's surreptitiously but as if under a compulsion pocketing a ripe pear without paying for it. Or it can be a brief sequence of action that pops into the head out of nowhere, from nothing seen or heard. Most of my germinal ideas are of the last type. For instance, the germ of the plot for *Strangers on a Train* was: "Two people agree to murder each other's enemy, thus permitting a perfect alibi to be established." The germinal idea for another book, *The Blunderer*, was not so promising, was more stubborn about developing, but showed a hardihood by sticking in my head for more than a year, and nagging at me until I found a way to write it. This was: "Two crimes are strikingly similar, though the people who commit them do not know each other." This idea would not interest many writers, I think. It is a "so what" idea. It needs embellishments and complications. In the book that resulted, I had the first crime done by a more or less cool killer, the second by an amateur attempting to copy the first, because he thinks the first killer has gotten away with his crime. Indeed, the first man would have, if not for the blundering effort of the second man to imitate him. And the second man did not even go through with his crime, only went to a certain point, a point at which the similarity was striking enough to attract the attention of a police detective. Thus a "so what" idea may have its variations.

Some story ideas never develop by parthenogenetic method, but need a second idea to get them going. One such ineffectual story germ was the original of *This Sweet Sickness*: "A man wants to cash in on the old insurance game, insuring himself, then apparently dying or disappearing, and finally collecting." There must be some way, I thought, to give this idea a new twist, to make it fresh and fascinating in a new kind of story. I labored over this for weeks in my evening hours. I wanted to have my criminal-hero set himself up in a different house with a different name, a house into which he could move permanently when his real self was presumably dead and gone. But the idea did not come to life. One day the second one appeared—in this case a far better motive than I had thought of until then, a love motive. The man was creating his second house for the girl he loved but never won, as the story turned out. He was not interested in insurance or money, because he had money. He was a man obsessed with his emotion. I wrote in my notebook under all my fruitless notes: "All the above is rot," and proceeded to work on my new line of thought. Everything came suddenly alive. It was a splendid feeling.

### The writer's imagination

Another story that needed two story germs to come alive was "The Terrapin," a short story which won a Mystery Writers of America award and has since been anthologized. The first germ came from a story a friend told me about someone she knew. One does not expect such stories to be fertile germs, because they are not one's own. The most exciting story told by a friend with the fatal remark, "I know you can make a terrific story out of this," is pretty sure to be of no value to the writer whatever. If it's a story, it's already a story. It doesn't need a writer's imagination, and his imagination and brain reject it artistically, as his flesh would reject the grafting of someone else's flesh upon it. A famous anecdote about Henry James relates that when a friend started to tell him "a story," James stopped him after a very few words. James had heard enough, and preferred to let his imagination do the rest.

However, this story: "A widow who is a commercial artist browbeats and pesters her ten-year-old son, makes him wear clothes too young for him, forces him to praise and admire her art work, and is generally turning the child into a tortured neurotic." Well, it was an interesting story, and my mother is a commercial artist (though not like this mother), and it did stay in my mind for about a year, though I never had an impulse to write it. Then one evening at someone's house, I was browsing in a cookbook and saw a horrifying recipe for cooking a terrapin stew. The recipe for turtle soup was hardly less grim, but at least one began the job by waiting until the turtle stuck his neck out and then coming down on it with a sharp knife. Readers who find that thrillers are beginning to pall may like to skim sections in cookbooks that have to do with our feathered and shelled friends; a housewife has to have a heart of stone to read these recipes, much less carry them out. The method of killing a terrapin was to boil it alive. The word killing was not used, and did not have to be, for what could survive boiling water?

As soon as I had read this, the story of the brow-beaten little boy came back to my mind. I would have the story turn upon a terrapin: the mother brings home a terrapin for a stew, a terrapin which the boy at first thinks is to be a pet for him. The boy tells one of his school friends about the terrapin, thereby trying to raise his status, and promises to show it. Then the boy witnesses the killing of the terrapin in boiling water, and all his pent-up resentment and hatred of his mother come out. He kills her in the middle of the night with the kitchen knife she had used to carve up the terrapin.

For months, maybe more than a year, I wanted to use a carpet as a means of concealment for a corpse, a carpet which perhaps someone carries in broad daylight, rolled up, out the front door of a house—ostensibly to the cleaners, while actually a corpse is inside it. I had not much doubt that this had been done. Someone told me, rightly or wrongly, that Murder, Inc. used such a means for getting some of their corpses from one place to another. Still, the idea interested me, and I tried to think how I could make the corpse-in-rug theme different and fresh and amusing. One obvious way was to have no corpse in it at all. In this case, the person carrying the carpet would have to be suspected of mur-der, would have to be seen carrying the carpet (perhaps in a furtive manner), would have to be a bit of a joker, in short. The germ was beginning to stir with life. I combined it with another tenuous idea I had about a writer-hero who finds a very thin and transparent line between his real life and the plots he dreams up, and gets the two a little mixed sometimes. This kind of writer-hero, I thought, could be not only amusing—and I mean in a comic sense—but could explore the rather harmless, everyday schizophrenia which everywhere abounds—yea, even in thee and me. The book that resulted was recently published as *The Story-Teller* in America and *A Suspension of Mercy* in England.

### Recognizing ideas

The germs of story ideas, then, can be little or big, simple or complex, fragmentary or rather complete, still or moving. The important thing is to recognize them when they come. I recognize them by a certain excitement which they instantly bring, akin to the pleasure and excitement of a good poem or line in a poem. Some things that appear to be plot ideas are not; they neither grow nor do they stay in the mind. Never mind, the world is full of germinal ideas, and they are countless as pebbles on a beach. It is not really possible to be out of ideas, since the ideas are all over the place, everywhere, just as usual. But there are several things that can cause a feeling of being "idea-less." One is physical and mental fatigue; because of pressures, some people are unable to remedy this very easily, even though they know how to and would if they could. The best way, of course, is to stop work and all thought of work and take a trip—even a short, cheap trip, just to change the scene. If you can't take a trip, take a walk. Some young writers drive themselves too hard, and in youth this works quite well, to a point. At that point, the unconscious rebels, the words refuse to come out, the ideas refuse to be born—the brain is demanding a vacation whether a vacation can be afforded or not. It is wise for a writer to have some sideline by which to earn some money, until he has enough books behind him to provide a constant trickle of income.

Another cause of this lack of ideas is the wrong kind of people around a writer, or sometimes people of any sort. People can be stimulating, of course, and a chance phrase, a piece of a story, can start the writer's imagination off. But mostly, the plane of social intercourse is not the plane of creation, not the plane on which creative ideas fly. It is difficult to be aware of, or receptive to, one's own unconscious when one is with a group of people, or even with a single person, though that is easier. This is a curious thing, because sometimes the very people we are attracted to or in love with act as effectively as rubber insulators to the spark of inspiration. I hope I will be forgiven for switching from bacteria to electricity in order to describe the creative process. It is difficult to describe. I also do not want to sound mystical about people and their effects on the writer, but there are some people, often most unlikely people—dull-witted, lazy, mediocre in every way—who are for some inexplicable reason stimulating to the imagination. I have known many such people. I like to see and talk to them now and then, if I can. It does not bother me that people may ask me, "What on earth do you see in X or Y?"

### Invisible antennae

I have never found other writers stimulating. I have heard other writers say the same thing, and I do not think it is because of jealousy or mistrust. I understand French writers usually do not feel this way and are fond of getting together to discuss their work. I cannot think of anything worse or more dangerous than to discuss my work with another writer. It would give me an uncomfortably naked feeling. It is a rather Anglo-Saxon and American attitude that a writer should keep his work to himself, and evidently I am stuck with it. I think the mutual discomfort among writers comes from the fact they are all somehow on the same plane, if they write fiction. Their invisible antennae are out for the same vibrations in the air—or to use a greedier metaphor, they swim along at the same depth, teeth bared for the same kind of drifting plankton. I get along much better with painters, and painting is the art most closely related to writing. Painters are accustomed to using their eyes, and it is good for a writer to do the same.

A germ of an idea, even if slight, often brings with it a most important factor for the final product, atmosphere. For instance, in *The Blunderer* germ (the similarity of two crimes), an atmosphere already hung about it, and it was one of gloom and defeatism. Whether I had set it in a rich or poor society, with young or old protagonists, the idea itself is a brooding, desperate and resourceless one, because a man who can think of nothing better than to imitate another, in crime, is essentially resourceless. It is also the plot for a hero who is doomed to failure and to tragedy.

One book of mine, *The Two Faces of January*, had particularly vague germinal ideas. Nevertheless, it turned into an entertaining book, and made the best-seller list in England. My impetus for this book was strong but quite fuzzy in the beginning. I wanted to write a book about a young, footloose American (I called him Rydal) in search of adventure, not a beatnik but a rather civilized and intelligent young man, and not a criminal, either. And I wanted to write about the effect on this young man of encountering a stranger who closely resembles his own domineering father. I had just made a trip to Greece and Crete in winter, and of course was strongly impressed by what I had seen. I remembered a musty old hotel I had stopped at in Athens, where the service was not very good, where the carpets were worn out, in whose corridors one heard a dozen different languages a day, and I wanted to use this hotel in my book. I wanted also to use the labyrinth at Knossos, which I had visited. While on this trip, I had been slightly rooked by a middle-aged man, a graduate of one of America's most esteemed universities. His highly respectable but weak face would be the face of my con man, Chester MacFarland, the man who resembled Rydal's genuinely respectable father, who was a professor.

Chester is married to a very pretty girl of the young American's age. With these few ingredients, I plunged into an adventure story with dash and gusto. The two young people are attracted to each other, but don't quite have an affair. She is killed accidentally by Chester, when Chester is attempting to kill Rydal. Chester and Rydal are then bound together by two and even three forces: one, that Rydal knows Chester has killed his own wife; two, that Rydal knows Chester has killed a police agent in Athens; and three, that Rydal has love-hate feelings toward Chester, because Chester resembles his father, and because Rydal is incapable of the unsportsmanlike step of simply turning Chester over to the police. Of course, things are not so simple in the book, as Chester manages to flee and hide from Rydal for a time. Chester is fleeing both Rydal and the law. It is the disintegration of Chester's character that we witness, and also Rydal's coming to terms with his own feeling toward his father—from whom he has suffered some rough treatment.

I highly recommend notebooks for writers, a small one if one has to be out on a job all day, a larger one if one has the luxury of staying at home. Even three or four words are often worth jotting down if they will evoke a thought, an idea or a mood. In the barren periods, one should browse through the notebooks. Some ideas may suddenly start to move. Two ideas may combine, perhaps because they were meant to combine in the first place.

# CHAPTER 2

## ✥ Mainly on Using Experiences

I feel I have been up to now setting down bits and pieces of information and suggestions which do not convey what it is really like to write a book. Perhaps that's impossible. And people have such different ways of working, of thinking out a story and characters. Above all, it is the impossibility of laying down rules that hampers me in writing about writing. I do not wish to lay down rules, so all I can do is suggest lines of approach to a book, some of which may be helpful to some people—and maybe others of no help to anybody.

The playwright Edward Albee says he thinks about his characters in a situation other than that of the play he has in mind, and if he can get them to behave properly or normally, he starts to write his play. Another successful playwright is furious with Aristotle for having said that a story needed a beginning, middle and an end. Albee's idea does not interest me, but it might interest other people. I know what the second playwright means, a play should start as near the end of its story as possible: that is an old law of the drama. In writing books, I compromise—consciously, because I have studied playwriting, and because I like a slow beginning.

### Momentum and conviction

To write a book and bring it off successfully means to acquire a certain momentum and drive and conviction which will last until the book is completed. I have also heard of writers who write a dramatic scene first, a scene that will come three-quarters of the way through their book. Who am I to say they are doing the wrong thing?

A book is not a thing of one sitting, like a poem, but a longish thing which takes time and energy, and since it takes skill, too, the first effort or maybe the second may not find a market. A writer should not think he is bad, or finished, if this happens, and of course writers with real drive will not. Every failure teaches something. You should have the feeling, as every experienced writer has, that there are more ideas where that one came from, more strength where the first strength came from, and that you are inexhaustible as long as you are alive. This requires an optimistic turn of mind, to say the least, and if you don't have it by nature, it has to be created artificially. You have to talk yourself into it sometimes. Psychologically speaking, a proper and decent period of mourning for a rejected manuscript is good—that is, one rejected about twenty times, really rejected, not just two or three times—but it shouldn't last more than a few days. You should not throw the manuscript out, either, because in one or two years you may know exactly what to do with it to make it sell.

To have the necessary momentum, that steady flow that is going to finish the book, you should wait until you feel the story welling up. This comes slowly during the development and plotting period, and you cannot rush it, because it is an emotional process, a sense of emotional completion, as if you felt like saying to yourself one day, "This is really a great story, and I can't wait to tell it!" Then you start writing.

### Record of emotional experience

I have said quite a bit about plots and gimmicks, and not enough about emotions, which play a part even in suspense writing. Good short stories are made from the writer's emotions alone, and their themes might often be equally well stated in poems. Even if a suspense book is entirely calculated, a product of the intellect, there will be scenes, descriptions of events—the sight of a dog being run over, a feeling of being followed in a dark street—which the writer has very likely known himself. The book is always better if there are first-hand and really felt experiences like these in it. It is part of the function of a notebook to hold a record of these things, emotional experiences, even if you don't have a fiction work in mind to attach them to when you write them down.

This might be described as the personal school of writing as opposed to the gimmick school. I think people are tired of gimmicks. Many people who don't write and who don't wish to write can come up with gimmicks. They are simply trick ideas, having nothing *per se* to do with literature or even prose, any more than practical jokes have. Some gimmicks are surprise endings; others a detail of medicine or chemistry unknown to the average layman which betrays or furthers the fortunes of the main character. Another type of gimmick is information withheld from the reader, quite arbitrarily and unfairly, until the end of the story or book. People who can't write very well can dress these gimmicks up in a bit of prose and sell them as short stories. There are many second- or third-string suspense stories printed every month in thirty-five cent magazines with gaudy names. They do not help much to give status to suspense and mystery writing.

*Ellery Queen's Mystery Magazine,* while it has its share of gimmicky material, is printing more and more stories of better quality, stories that are simply good stories and good entertainment, rather than suspense or mystery stories. Back to the old cliché that all stories have suspense. *Ellery Queen's Mystery Magazine* is putting the theory into practice.

Recently I was surprised that *Ellery Queen's Mystery Magazine* bought a story of mine called "Another Bridge to Cross." I wrote the story on a weekend in Rome, to vary the monotony of writing *The Glass Cell,* which I worked on during weekdays. The story was based on: 1) my hearing a slow song played by a guitar on someone's gramophone in Positano, a song with a long melody line which I had not heard before and have not heard since; and 2) the remark of a sociologist friend in Rome that many poor Italian men commit suicide because the State will give a small income to their wives and children if they are dead. I was impressed and touched by both these things. The song stayed in my mind, redolent of southern Italy and the Mediterranean beaches there. At any rate, in my Rome apartment, nearly out of my mind from lack of sleep, since from 5 A.M. to 7 A.M. were the only reasonably quiet hours in my neighborhood, I began to write a story for my own pleasure, not caring if it ever sold or not.

The story was about a middle-aged American named Merrick, touring Europe alone to try to get over his grief after his wife's death. It begins as he is driving in a chauffeured car up the west coast of the Riviera. A man, standing quietly on a bridge that spans the road, jumps to his death just after Merrick's car passes. Later, when Merrick is installed in a hotel in Positano, he reads of the suicide in a newspaper and sends a money order for a large sum, anonymously, to the man's widow— for the dead man is one of the poor who has killed himself to bring a little money to his starving family.

Meanwhile, Merrick makes the acquaintance of a small street boy whom he invites to dinner at his hotel, and during the evening, the boy robs the pocketbook of a wealthy American woman. The money order is returned to Merrick unopened, because the Italian widow has committed suicide out of grief and killed her children with her. Thus Merrick's two quiet but desperate attempts to make contact with the human race again, through friendliness and kindness, are thrown back in his face. It drives him farther into the lonely, melancholic, mist-shrouded world within himself, composed of his memories of his happier past which he cannot relate to the present. He sits for hours in the hotel garden. A guitar somewhere plays the song with the long melody line which reminds Merrick of a song he and his wife heard on their honeymoon in Amalfi. The hotel manager at last summons a doctor, knowing Merrick is not right in his head, and Merrick bestirs himself to move on from the town on the next leg of his planned journey northward.

He is a man in a fog, and the fog is becoming thicker. This is a tragic story, one could hardly call it a "suspense" story, and there is no violent action in it, except the suicide on the bridge at the beginning. It is a story written from my own emotions, because I wanted to write it. I sent it to my agent with a note, "I can't think of a market for this, but maybe you can." *Ellery Queen's Mystery Magazine* published it.*

### The start of a story

Part of the time I was working on *Deep Water,* I lived in a cold-water flat on East 56th Street in Manhattan, on the first floor, and my back window had a fire escape with a ladder that led to the ground ten feet below. One day shortly after I had moved in, I entered the apartment and saw five or six boys, aged about fifteen and younger, hunched over my books and paint boxes which I had not yet put away. They rushed past me in a fast stream down the hall and out the door. I had left the window slightly open, and they had come in from the fire escape. I erased with turpentine the daubs they made on one of my suitcases. It was a dis-

* Reprinted in Ellery Queen's 20th Anniversary Annual.

turbing experience. On another day, I was at my desk working when I heard yelling and shouting, and a great clanging of shoes on iron, and the boys started a free-for-all on the fire escape only two yards from where I sat. Absent-mindedly, I retreated, and a few seconds later was amused to find myself standing in the far corner of the room like a scared rat, still frowning with concentration as I tried to compose the last half of the sentence that was in the typewriter across the room.

I do not understand people who like to make noise; consequently I fear them, and since I fear them, I hate them. It is a vicious emotional cycle. On this occasion, my heart was beating absurdly fast, and I waited until the boys had decided to leave, as I was much too cowardly to speak to them. I might certainly call this an "emotional experience."

Several months later, I was inspired as a result of this to write a short story called "The Barbarians." A young architect with overtime work is tortured by the noise of soccer players in a vacant lot below his window every Saturday and Sunday afternoon. The players reply to his requests for less noise with taunts and insults, and the architect reaches such a pitch of nerves that he drops an eight-pound stone on the head of one of the players in the lot. The architect ducks back. The injured man is carried away but returns the next day to play with a bandaged head. But the police do not arrive. The architect is only heckled after that: his windows are broken when he comes home from work; there is chewing gum in his doorlock; and he is mildly beaten up when he encounters a couple of the players at

night. The architect is afraid to ask for police help, because what he did was more serious than their heckling.
The story ended with the situation unresolved. It did
not sell anywhere at first.

I expanded it with a movie scenario in mind, set
it in Italy, and had the injured player die from his skull
fracture. Officially, this is reported as an accident: The
player is said to have run against a wall. The group of
sportsmen want to reserve the architect as their special
prey, without interference from the police. The architect knows that the injured player died, and he is afraid
to bring the police into the matter. A neighbor has wit-
nessed the rock-dropping, and gently but effectively
blackmails the architect, who has no alternative but to
pay him. When the architect marries, his young wife is
heckled also. She notices a shortage of money in the
household, and the architect is forced to tell her the
horrible story. She advises him to stop paying the blackmailer, who she says will never go to the police. The
architect does refuse to make the next payment, and the
blackmailer walks away in the direction of the police
station. This scene is watched by the ever-lurking soccer
player or two, who realize exactly what is happening.
This is their last chance to get a whack in before the
police come on the scene, so they surround the architect,
hustle him into an alley, and murder him.

This story almost, but not quite, interested an Italian
movie director enough to buy. "The Barbarians" saw the
first light of print in French, in an anthology of short
stories by several authors. Later it was included in

my book of short stories called *The Snail-Watcher*. I tell this story as an example of what can be done with small personal experiences—if they are emotional ones. It is amusing to let the imagination play with such incidents as a faintly heard song and an invaded apartment, and to see what evolves from them.

Other experiences are quieter. My grandmother died some years ago. I was very fond of her, and she had most of the job of raising me until I was six, as my mother was busy with her work. There was little or no resemblance between me and my grandmother, though of course she gave me some of the bones and blood that I have, and our hands were a little alike. Not long ago, I happened to glance at a nearly worn-out shoe of mine which had taken the shape of my foot, and there I saw the shape, or expression, of my grandmother's foot, as I remembered it from her house slippers and from the low-heeled black pumps she used to wear when she went out. I was reminded of the time when I was seventeen, visiting my grandmother in Texas in an interval between high school and college, when we went to the film of "A Midsummer-Night's Dream".

My grandmother suffered from cataracts in her later years (she lived until I was thirty-four), but this never kept her from enjoying life, or from taking a lively interest in books, the theatre and movies, embroidery and quilting, gardening and her produce from it. I remembered how thrilled I was that evening we went across town, by taxi, to see "A Midsummer-Night's Dream" at some huge but remote movie house, since this bill of fare was not popular enough for mid-town Fort Worth houses. I remembered my grandmother's very firm grip on my arm as we walked to our seats, and her feeling along with her feet, even though I warned her when we were at a step. We always made quite good progress, though my grandmother would be concentrating already on whatever was on the screen, whether it was the newsreel or a cartoon. I thought that evening, "Mendelssohn was no older than I when he wrote that overture. What a genius!" And my heart was very full of good things that evening. When I saw my old shoe twenty years later, I shed the first real tears for my grandmother, realized her death for the first time, her long life, her absence now, and I realized also my own death to come.

### Positive or negative emotions

It is out of such emotions as these that good short stories are made, but I never wrote one about this. If I ever write about my grandmother, it will have to be very good or not at all. It is much easier to create from positive, affectionate emotions than from negative and hateful ones. Jealousy, while powerful, I find of no use at all, and it most resembles the disease cancer, eating away and giving nothing. On the other hand, look what Shakespeare did with it in *Othello*, or rather Giraldi Cinthio before him, but it was Shakespeare who put the flesh on the plot, as Cinthio's characters are said to be only "faintly indicated."

The vast majority of people are capable of emotional experiences like these, both great and small. The writer

will seize on even the smallest, and turn it to use if he
can. These experiences might also be called emotional
buffetings of one kind or another, and God knows they
are not always pleasant. They go on from the cradle to
the grave. Some people build a shell to protect themselves from various buffetings. It may be called, in some
people, decorum or training, and often with it goes the
ability to turn aside an insult or to inflict one without
mercy, the ability to conceal, destroy and forget an emotion if it is not a proper emotion to feel. With practice,
these people can become almost immune to any emotion.

To feel emotion, it is not necessary to show it, of
course, and in fact showing it may lose a little of it,
from a creative point of view. But among the conceal-
ers, a moral judgment is often passed automatically,
and the impact goes by them, as it were. Creative people
do not pass moral judgments—at least not at once—on
what meets their eye. There is time for that later in
what they create, if they are so inclined, but art essentially has nothing to do with morality, convention or
moralizing.

Another type of protection is an acquired blindness
or indifference that may be found, for instance, in some
people who work on farms or in poor communities
where death is an everyday thing. Obviously, it makes
life easier not to think about or become attached to an
animal, if one is going to have to kill it oneself in six
months, and not to think about the pain of hunger and
cold and death, if one is going to be jogged by the sight
of it every hour of the day.

### Receptivity and awareness

The majority of people are nowhere near these two extremes of self-protectiveness. Artists born into the families of either type may break out of these patterns. Robert Burns remained a farmer, but one who was so upset at ruining a mouse's burrow with his plough-share, that he was moved to write a poem about it. Writers and painters have by nature little in the way of protective shells and try all their lives to remove what they have, since various buffetings and impressions are the material they need to work from. This receptivity, this awareness of life, is an artist's ideal, and takes precedence over all his activities and attitudes; this is why creative people are called, sociologically, classless. Because they are alike and understand one another in this fundamental matter, they usually mix easily, whatever their backgrounds.

# CHAPTER 3

## ✎ THE SUSPENSE SHORT STORY

THE suspense short story and also the mystery-detective short story is lately cropping up everywhere. Anthony Boucher in his *Best Detective Stories of the Year* (1964) cites one from *Bridge World* ("of all places to find a detective story") in his honor list, which goes to prove that if a story is good entertainment, everyone will enjoy it—bridge players as well as mystery and suspense fans. For writers with fertile imaginations and quick typewriters, suspense short story writing is a splendid way to increase income and spread fame.

**Compared to the novel . . .**

To start with basic things, what is the difference between a suspense short story and a suspense novel? The suspense novel usually, though not always, covers a longer span of time: the nature of the germ of the idea necessitates this. In the novel, there is often also a drastic change in the hero or heroine, and maybe in several characters: their characters develop, change, improve or collapse. There are probably more changes of scene.

The story line is longer: the climax or climaxes cannot be reached by the springboard of merely one preceding scene, or a single scene itself. There is time for change of mood and change of pace. There is scope for more than one viewpoint. All these possibilities of the suspense novel are not necessarily present in every suspense novel, and in fact should be present only when fitting and contributory to the plot and to what one wants to say. They are not essential ingredients, only characteristics.

The suspense short story germ may well start with the flimsiest fact, event or possibility—such as crucial fingerprints being washed off a cocktail glass by rain on a terrace. A suspense short story may have only one scene and take place in five minutes or less. It may be based on an emotional situation or incident—such as the hunting (by one man) of a mysterious animal which is terrorizing the neighborhood, and which only one man, the hero, is brave enough to pursue. The suspense short story (like many a detective short story) may be based on a gimmick, a tricky means of escape (from any place), or a piece of information known mostly only by doctors, lawyers or astronauts that will surprise and amuse the layman. Bits of unusual information that a writer may come upon while browsing through technical books can often be the nucleus of a story which will sell and provide a few minutes' entertainment for the reader. Obviously, this is the reverse of the emotional or inspirational method of creating a story, since the odd bit of information, the curious fact, is perceived through the eyes and is not immediately connected with characters who are going to use it. These germs are potentialities, not alive until characters make them alive. I don't think much of this kind of writing (I don't know who does), but I have now and then done it when an amusing idea came my way.

For instance, the fingerprints washed off the cocktail glass by the rain. In a big novel, this could be a serious matter somewhere in the plot, but I wasn't writing a novel at the time the thought came to me. I saw it only as a possible short story, and as something an anxious, nail-chewing murderer could not prevent, because he could not reach the terrace. My story was called "You Can't Depend on Anybody," and appeared in *Ellery Queen's Mystery Magazine*. A jealous, washed-up, middle-aged actor plants the murder of his mistress (which he has done himself) on her new boy friend, whose fingerprints are on one of the glasses on the terrace of her house. The middle-aged actor is frantic for the superintendent of the apartment house, for the police, for a friend—anybody—to open the apartment and find the body, but three days pass. He can stir up no alarm in the superintendent's mind, not enough to make him unlock the door. A heavy rain comes, and that is the end of the fingerprints. The actor is caught, because he has carefully put on the corpse a wide silver bracelet which his mistress habitually wore, and which he thought would make her look more natural. His fingerprints are on the bracelet. The entertainment in the story comes from the efforts of the actor to combat the well-known reluctance of New Yorkers to invade an apartment, however silent it is. "You can lie there dead for days and no one will," etc.

A better story, still with a surprise trap-for-the-hero at the end, is "Man in Hiding" by Vincent Starrett, in *Ellery Queen's Mystery Magazine*. A doctor has killed his wife. Under another name, two months prior to the murder, he has rented an office in which he intends to set up a rare book business—all this by way of hiding out until he can join his girl friend Gloria in Paris. The doctor is extremely nervous, though all is going fairly well. He is very suspicious of a private investigator's office in his building. It seems to him that they are watching him. The doctor has made the acquaintance of a girl who runs an antique shop in the building, and there is a large Spanish chest in her reception room. It has crossed the doctor's mind that the chest would be a good place to hide, in case the police actually invade his office. Mr. Starrett improves the suspense by describing a couple of narrow squeaks the doctor has with former patients who pass him in the street. One day, the police do call on him. The doctor has just time to dart to the antique shop and jump, unseen, into the chest—which closes with a click. The reader knows that the police have come simply to sell tickets for a benefit affair. And the reader knows also that the girl who runs the antique shop has in mind to open that old chest one day, once she gets around to it, but not for a very long time. This could be a poor story, told by an incompetent writer. Vincent Starrett has made the most of it, written it well and convincingly, and also briefly, in about two thousand words.

A quite well-done gimmick story in the same issue of *Ellery Queen's Mystery Magazine* is Cornell Woolrich's "Murder after Death." The gimmick is that an injection into a corpse stays put, because the circulatory system is no longer functioning. Mr. Woolrich has created an elaborate but quite entertaining and believable scaffolding for this: A medical student who has been washed out of school is in a rage because his girl friend has married another. His beloved dies as a result of a chill that has led to pneumonia. He very much wants to put the blame on her young husband, so he visits the corpse in the funeral parlor and injects her with poison. He manages to plant a vial of the same poison in the hotel bedroom of the despondent young husband. Then he spreads the news, by anonymous letter, that the girl was murdered. He confidently expects an exhumation which will put the blame on the husband, but the husband commits suicide, thus thwarting his desire for vengeance. And a medical examination reveals that the poison was injected after death. The story is strengthened by the introduction of the young husband as an important character and an appealing one.

Looking through the *Best Detective Stories*, which I read for the first time less than a year ago, I was surprised and a little depressed to realize how few of even the "best" stay in my mind. I remembered best Borden Deal's "The Cattywampus," which is about a hunter who accepts the challenge of pursuing with rifle a strange beast that is frightening the district. The hunter finds to his amazement a huge old bear, scarred by battle and brushfire, clawless and unable even to catch fish for food any longer. He shoots him out of pity. The story is serious and moving the whole way, but it is the end which gives the story its value and makes it memorable:

> . . . I would go back into the valley and I would tell them, in order to remove the fear, that I had killed the strange animal. But I would also tell them that his body had gone into the river and I had not been able to identify it. For I knew now. Mankind needs its strange animals, its myths and legends and old tales, in order to objectify man's fears outside of himself where he can fight them with man's courage and man's hope.
> For man is the strangest animal of all.

The bit I have quoted might be called a comment by the writer. It is not necessary to the action, but it is a thought. It gives the story a dignity and importance it would not otherwise have. It is the kind of thought a poet might have, if he were writing a poem of this story, but there is nothing "poetic" about this thought, it is simply intelligent. And it is, for me, the thing that made this story stand out among sixteen others which were merely entertaining. This story is from *Argosy*. Of the others, three are from *Alfred Hitchcock's Mystery Magazine*, five from *Ellery Queen's Mystery Magazine*, one from *The Saturday Evening Post*, one from *This Week*, two from *Playboy*, one each from *The Saint*, *Manhunt*, *Rogue*, and *Fantastic*.

### The "quick" novel

The suspense novelette falls between the short story and the novel in regard to the characteristics of each that I mentioned. There is scope in the novelette, so much that one might call it a "quick" novel, or a telescoped novel. I mean the eighty-page or twenty-thousand-word length. Some magazines call twelve thousand words a novelette, but this is a category that has never been strictly defined as to word-number. One should ascertain the exact required length when aiming at a magazine market. It is a very profitable market, if one has the knack. For a one-shot eighty-page suspense novelette, the price is five or more times the advance for a full-length suspense novel. But it seems to me that quite as much thought has to be put into a novelette as into a full-length novel. The mass of prose may not be in the novelette, but the change in character and characters, changes of scene, changes of viewpoint, may well be. The action must move faster than the action of a novel, which means that the same amount of action is there, but told in briefer form.

I was once asked to try an eighty-page original for *Cosmopolitan*. I had never tried creating anything in this way, on order, as it were, but I gave it a try by sitting with pencil and paper and racking my brains for an idea. I came up with two ideas:

1) A man and wife vacationing in Mexico. The wife wants to get rid of the tedious husband, and so asks him to "take another step back" as he is standing at the edge

of a precipice, trying to snap a picture of her. She has to give him a slight push, finally, and at the same moment the camera snaps, and is lost with the husband down a ravine so deep that only the "authorities" can reach the bottom. The camera recorded the misdeed. This story, in synopsis, was much more complicated and not quite as bad as it sounds here, but was nonetheless rejected.

2) A newly married couple, the girl rich, take their honeymoon in a country cottage belonging to the girl's family. The husband has a girl friend on the side, and his plan is to kill his wife for her money and marry the girl friend. The wife, a nervous type, thinks she misses food from the kitchen and that she hears noises in the cellar. When the husband investigates the cellar, he finds a fugitive from the law in hiding. He immediately sees that he can make use of the fugitive, promises not to betray him, and says he will bring him food. The husband reports to his wife that there is nothing in the cellar, that she is imagining the noises. This situation continues for several days. The husband plots with the fugitive: The fugitive must pretend to hold up the cottage, and the husband will permit him (by pretending to be knocked out) to leave the cottage and make his escape in the husband's car. The husband really means to kill his wife and blame it on the not-too-bright fugitive. The wife discovers the man in the cellar and learns of her husband's plan. She then plots with the fugitive against the husband, turning the tables.

This synopsis was also received coolly at *Cosmopolitan,* and was never written as a novelette, but was bought for television and performed in 1956. Ten years later, in England, the BBC saw the old script, liked the story and bought it also. I had to rewrite it completely, remove the platitudes and old-fashionedness of 1956, and generally make it more sophisticated. It will also be sold to German television. The moral to this anecdote is, never throw away a story with a good story line, even in synopsis. The story is a "suspense" story as soon as we know the husband and wife are alone in a cottage and that he intends to kill her. But the surprise of finding a criminal lurking in the cellar, a violent man whom the husband is determined to protect, is the making of the story, tremendously heightening the suspense. Without this, the story would be just another story of potential violence, like thousands of others.

Novelists—most of them—have a lot of ideas that are brief and minor, that cannot or should not be made into books. They may make good or spectacularly good short stories. Some are of a fantastic nature, involving time-machines, the supernatural. A writer couldn't perhaps entertain himself or a reader with two hundred and forty pages of such fantasy, but everyone may be pleased by ten pages. I know of novelists who throw short story ideas away, and never even jot them down. I think suspense novelists are not so cramped in this respect, and are apt to be more flexible imaginatively than straight novelists, perhaps because they do not put themselves on a very lofty plane.

Write down all these slender ideas. It is surprising

how often one sentence, jotted in a notebook, leads immediately to a second sentence. A plot can develop as you write notes. Close the notebook and think about it for a few days—and then presto! you're ready to write a short story.

# CHAPTER 4

## ⚓ DEVELOPMENT

BY *development,* I mean the process that must take place between the germ of a story and the detailed plotting. And that is a great deal. For me, it can take from six weeks to three years, not three years of constant work, but three years of slow brewing while I am working on other things.

The idea must be fleshed with characters, with setting, with atmosphere. One must know what these characters look like, how they dress and talk, and one should know even about their childhoods, though their childhoods do not always need to be written into the book. All this is a matter of living with one's characters and in their setting for some period of time before writing the first word. The setting and the people must be seen as clearly as a photograph—with no foggy spots. Besides this formidable task, the themes or lines of action must be contemplated, juggled around, combined to bring out the most in them. As I write this, I am reminded of the old alchemists' vague recipes: "Stir pot ten times to the right, five times to the left, but only if the spring moon is at its height, and only if a thin black cloud like a cat's tail passes from right to left across the face of the moon," etc. What is the height of the moon? What month in spring? What is the improvement of a plot?

### Thickening the plot

The improvement or thickening of a plot is the piling on of complications for the hero, or perhaps for his enemies. These complications are most effective in the form of surprise events. If the writer can thicken the plot and surprise the reader, the plot is logically improved. But you cannot always create a good book by sheer logic. Some excellent plots are very simple: a direct flight-and-pursuit plot, for instance, or a plot that consists merely of the story of a woman who cannot get herself to the point of murdering her husband, though she wants to—a story of indecision. This skeleton of "indecision" is simplicity itself. Literally nothing happens, and yet in the course of the story you might—just *might*—pile complication upon complication: unexpected people arriving to interrupt the murderess, a letter from someone in her family rousing fears of an eternal punishment if she does the deed. There is room for comedy and tragedy here, as there is in nearly every plot.

I can give no advice, or do not presume to give any, on the question of concentrating on character or plot in the course of developing a story idea. I have concentrated on either or both. Most often for me comes a short bit of action, with no characters attached, which will be the hub or the climax, occasionally the start, of my story. Obviously, sometimes a character full of quirks will by those quirks give initial action to the plot. In other situations, it is just as plain that an unusual situation must lead to other unusual situations— that is, advancement in action—and then the character or characters are not so "important" in the plot's progress. I see no reason why letting plot or character take the lead in plotting should be held inferior or superior to the opposite method.

Occasionally, I use a character "from real life," in the sense that I use the physical appearance of someone I have met. I have never used both the physical appearance and the personality of anyone I knew, but often have used appearance with a different personality. There are two reasons for this: one, I would be very shy about using both appearance and personality, or writing a literal portrait of someone; and two, I meet many people whose faces are quickly learned but whose characters are not· known in a profound sense. And naturally the internal character one needs for a book is not often found ready-made in real life.

I imagine that most suspense writers begin with a germ of an idea which is a piece of action, and this generally has a setting: the New York business world; a boat at sea; a small town in America; a lumber camp; a government spy headquarters. The setting will very much govern the kind of characters you will use. But it might improve your story to use a character not at all typical of this setting, not at all a person one might expect to find in such an environment. There is a limit as to how far one can go with incongruities, but the result, if it comes off, is more interesting than the typical.

Let us take a look at the development of *The Story-Teller* from those two fuzzy story germs of corpse-in-the-carpet and a writer-hero-who-gets-plots-mixed-with-real-life. Once I had decided to combine these two ideas, the book had a gestation period of only five or six weeks, and it took four months to write—a record short time for me. Since I had been living in Suffolk (England), I wanted to use this new ground and atmosphere and set the book there. I am not so comfortable writing about the English as I am about the Americans, so I made my hero a young American married to an English girl and living in the country, as I do. And because I was interested in showing the American's everyday or garden variety of schizophrenia in an amusing way, I made him a novelist who is currently trying to write for television—so his head is full of episodes for a television series called "The Whip," which he has conceived and is trying to sell.

### Crucial questions

Early in development, the writer must ask these crucial questions: "Is the hero going to emerge from this victor or vanquished?" And, "Is the atmosphere one of comedy, tragedy, or both mixed? Or is it a kind of flat reporting of events and cruel fate for the reader to make of what he wishes?" Your prose must have an atmosphere, just as a physical scene must have. My hero,

Sydney, would emerge if not exactly victor, certainly not victim or vanquished. The tone would be light. Sydney was not to be punished or caught, and in fact I thought it would be interesting to have him commit no crime at all, only be suspected of one or two. The book did not turn out quite this way. Sydney does at last commit an odd murder, which he thinks of as a temporary "suspension of mercy" on his part. He kills his wife's lover by forcing him to take an overdose of sleeping pills. But Sydney is only slightly suspected of this, and nothing can be proven.

In brief, the plot is: Sydney's wife, Alicia, goes for the second time to Brighton for a few days, "for a change of scene," and the morning after her departure, Sydney acts out an idea he has long had. He pretends he pushed Alicia down the stairs the day before, and at dawn he carries a rolled carpet out the back door, puts it into his car, and buries the carpet in the woods. He thinks he may be able to use his imagined feelings at some time when he is writing fiction. He of course expects his wife to return home after a few days, but she doesn't, because she has begun an affair with a London lawyer in Brighton. The reader knows this, but Sydney does not. A nice old lady named Mrs. Lilybanks, who lives two hundred yards away from Sydney and Alicia, has seen the carpet-carrying, and eventually reports it to the police. The police are unable to find Alicia, because she is using another name in Brighton and has also dyed her hair. Sydney is put under surveillance. Believing that his wife is quite safe, wherever she is, Sydney does not mind the police questioning, but indeed enjoys it, because he is imagining what his feelings would be if he *were* guilty of having murdered Alicia. Sydney can make himself actually tremble and perspire under police interrogation—and later he takes notes on himself for his own use. He at last discovers, by going to Brighton and searching the area, that his wife is alive and is sharing a cottage with a man. This shakes him up, and he rightly guesses that it has shaken his wife up, too; because she is essentially strait-laced. Alicia cannot reveal herself to the police or face her parents or Sydney, and she commits suicide by throwing herself over a cliff near Brighton. The lawyer boy friend retreats hastily to London and his own apartment, but Sydney seeks him out there and administers the fatal dose of sleeping pills.

I have outlined the plot to show that it is not much without the thickening, or the pointing up. There were four thickening factors:

1) Mrs. Lilybanks, the neighbor, has acquired a pair of binoculars from a second-hand shop, as she is a bird-watcher. Sydney discovers that she has binoculars, and correctly guesses that she may have seen him the morning he took the rolled carpet out of the house and drove off with it. Sydney's "reaction" to the binoculars increases Mrs. Lilybanks' suspicion of him.

2) Mrs. Lilybanks has a weak heart. She is a nice old lady, who informed the police only after much hesitation that her next-door neighbor carried a carpet out of his house at dawn the morning after his wife presuma-

bly left for Brighton. The police dig nearly twenty-four hours in the woods, as Sydney cannot remember the exact spot at which he buried the carpet, though he is trying to be cooperative. At last the news comes that the police have found the carpet with nothing in it, and Sydney goes to Mrs. Lilybanks' house to bring her this reassuring information. But Mrs. Lilybanks thinks that Sydney is going to be angry and resentful, and she suffers a fatal heart attack when she hears him entering her house. Sydney is therefore under a new suspicion: that he threatened or in some way expressed hostility against Mrs. Lilybanks in retaliation for her having told the police about the carpet.

3) Sydney has an informal writing partner named Alex, a married man who lives in London. When "The Whip" series is bought for television, Alex would very much like to force Sydney out of the contract and reap all the gains himself, and he has some hope of doing this because of the suspicion that Sydney is under. Alex paints his erstwhile friend in the worst possible light to the police. And to this is added the suspension of a book contract by Sydney's publishers "until the mystery of your wife's disappearance is cleared up."

4) Sydney loses his small notebook one day when he is buying a newspaper in his village. The shopkeeper turns the notebook over to the police. In this notebook, Sydney is keeping his thoughts on how it feels to be a murderer, and his narration of his wife's "murder" reads like something in a diary. Thus I piled the pressure on Sydney.

### A sense of life

When I began to write this book, I had gotten no further in my plotting than the period of Mrs. Lilybanks' indecision as to whether or not to say she saw Sydney carrying a carpet out of his house. This was perhaps around page one hundred and twenty. I often reach a point beyond which I cannot think, cannot make an outline, and I become impatient to see something on paper, and so I begin—and I trust to my luck, or to the momentum of the story, to carry me on. This may sound as if I am very vague, but what I wait for is a sense of life, of activity, of something dynamic in the characters and setting of the first section of the book, action that I can clearly see and feel. This is not a vague sensation at all. There is absolutely no doubt when it is there, and no doubt when it is not there. I do not start writing with a hope that it will come. It must be there, and by its stirring with life, it will stir me to begin writing.

A plot, after all, should never be a rigid thing in the writer's mind when he starts to work. I carry this thought one step further and believe that a plot should not even be completed. I have to think of my own entertainment, and I like surprises myself. If I know everything that is going to happen, it is not so much fun writing it. But more important is the fact that a flexible plot line lets the characters move and make decisions like living people, gives them a chance to debate with themselves, make choices, take them back, make others, as people do in real life. Rigid plots, even if perfect, may result in a cast of automatons.

After I reached page one hundred and twenty or so, Mrs. Lilybanks' period of indecision, the story rolled on easily to page two hundred and thirty, where I struck a hitch of indecision. Was Sydney really to commit a murder or pretend again to have done so? What kind of person was Sydney, anyway? He was certainly developing in the course of the book, both to me and to himself. He had come to the conclusion, in his small notebook, that he could not imagine fully the sensations of a murderer. With Sydney, a sense of guilt is in the way— a feeling of shame, of being cut off from the human race. Sydney, in short, is not a murderer, and he knows he has failed (as an imaginative writer) to imagine a murderer's state of mind. Nevertheless, his effort at imagining has brought him closer to the real thing, closer to the act. Using the sleeping pills, Sydney does perform the strange slow murder of a man he detests, and who he believes has caused his wife's death. It is a crime, and the beginning of a possibly more serious muddle in Sydney's mind between his plots and reality.

Plot-thickening factors might also be called bolsterings of the plot. One should invent the most logical (since they are invented, they are apt to be a bit illogical per se, and this is an advantage), those which make the story more believable and stronger. It is possible to invent twenty or thirty bolsterings sometimes, but then you would have the reader laughing instead of being convinced.

**Likable criminals**

There are many kinds of suspense books—government spy stories, for instance—which do not depend on psychopathic or neurotic heroes like mine. For writers who wish to write books similar to mine, there is an added problem, that of how to make the hero likable, or even reasonably so. This is often damnably difficult. Though I think all my criminal heroes are fairly likable, or at least not repugnant, I must admit I have failed to make some of my readers think so, if I am to go by remarks made to me about them: "I found Ripley (*The Talented Mr. Ripley*) interesting, I suppose, but I really hated him. Ugh!" "I hated Walter (*The Blunderer*). He's so weak and full of self-pity." So far, the readers of *The Story-Teller* seem to like Sydney quite well, but then he is not a psychopath, and barely a murderer. I can only suggest giving the murderer-hero as many pleasant qualities as possible—generosity, kindness to some people, fondness for painting or music or cooking, for instance. These qualities can also be amusing in contrast to his criminal or homicidal traits.

I think it is also possible to make a hero-psychopath one hundred percent sick and revolting, and still make him fascinating for his very blackness and all-round depravity. I very nearly did this with Bruno in *Strangers on a Train*, for even Bruno's generosity is neither consistent nor well-placed, and there is nothing else to be said in his favor. But in that story, Bruno's evil was offset by Guy's "goodness," which considerably simplified the problem I had of providing a likable hero, as Guy became the likable hero. It depends on the writer's skill, whether he can have a frolic with the evil in his hero-psychopath. If he can, then the book is entertaining, and in that case there is no reason why the reader should have to "like" the hero. If there must be reader-identification, a term I am rather tired of, then provide the reader with a lesser character or two (preferably one who is not murdered by the hero-psychopath) with whom he can identify.

## Quest and development

The development of a story idea is as much creative as finding or receiving it initially. A writer can apply his thinking powers to developing the story germ, but the brain in such a process has a function more of excluding (because of illogic) than of including or inventing anything. With a gimmick, a germ of an idea, or a brief action sequence, a writer may think of five or six situations that could lead up to it or follow it (developing a story idea is a back-and-forth process, like weaving), and he might eliminate three of these situations as being illogical or simply not as good as the other three. Then he may experience the depressing sensation of the remaining three situations not coming alive, not being inspiring—of standing still. He throws the pencil down and leaves the desk with a feeling that not much has been accomplished that day, that perhaps the idea is dead anyway. And then later, when he is not thinking about the story at all, one of these motionless ideas will come alive and start to move, and will advance itself—and suddenly he has a whole stretch of good narrative. Archimedes was in his bathtub, when he shouted "Eureka!", not bending over his problem at his desk, or whatever he used. But such moments of glory do not come unless you have stewed over the problem beforehand.

Though this is hard work indeed, because it seems profitless, it is preparing the ground for the imagination to do the rest. My notebooks are filled with pages, perhaps twenty or more for each book I have written, which are simply tangential or fantastic rambles around the germ or the main action or situation, which is the only thing that remained constant in the developing process. These divagations usually bear no resemblance to the final book. But they are necessary for the better ideas that come later; these I usually do not bother writing down because they are obviously right and unforgettable.

Edna O'Brien, a talented young Irish novelist, said in an interview, "Writers are always working. They never stop." This is the nature of the job of writing, at least of writing fiction. Writers are either developing an idea or they are questing, even if unconsciously, for the germ of an idea.

I create things out of boredom with reality and with the sameness of routine and objects around me. Therefore, I don't dislike this boredom which encroaches on me every now and then, and I even try to create it by routine. I do not "have to work" in the sense that I must drive myself to it or make myself think what to do, because the work will come to me. I get the same pleasure from making a table, a good drawing, occasionally a painting, as I do from writing a book or a short story. This boredom is a happy thing, and I am scarcely aware of it until an idea for a short story or a book strikes me. Then I realize how much more interesting I shall find the world I enter when I start working on this idea. I am already entering that world when I start thinking about the development of the idea. Perhaps most writers feel this way.

The developing of an idea is often not at all logical, and there is such an element of play in it, I can't call the process a serious activity, though it may involve spots of hard thinking. It is still part of a game. Writing fiction is a game, and one must be amused all the time to do it. The only times that are not amusing to me, perhaps, come when I have to work under difficulties, to meet a severe deadline. Deadlines seldom occur in book-writing, but they do in television work, in writing condensations of one's own work, or in making changes in a book scheduled to appear in serial form.

## Distractions and directions

As for life's little difficulties, they are myriad. What writer hasn't had to work with a toothache, with bills due, with a baby sick in the next room or the same room, with the in-laws visiting, or at the end of a love affair, or with the government demanding the filling out of endless forms? I have scarcely a morning that doesn't bring something in the post that could be called psychically disturbing. I have never been sued for libel, neither have I any debts, but there are other things that can plague a writer—the insistence of the government that a writer estimate his income for the coming year, a thing impossible to do; news of the loss or appropriation of possessions brought about by moving or traveling from one place or country to the other (writers are often traveling because they need changes of scene); or difficulties in finding a dwelling place. Once when I had everything settled about a new apartment in Manhattan —advance rent paid, the lease signed, the movers ready —I was informed that I could not have it because it was a professional apartment. Writers are not professionals, because "their clients do not come to them." I thought of writing to the Department of Housing or whoever made this law, "You have no idea how many characters ring my doorbell and come to me every day, and I absolutely need them for my existence," but I never wrote this, only reflected that prostitutes could probably qualify, but writers couldn't.

Then to trouble the mind further, there are the eternal maneuverings one has to perform in order to exist on an irregular and often inadequate income, irksome to people by nature not inclined to economy, much less to cheeseparing—the insecurity that is the very air writers breathe, since they are in a profession without unemployment insurance, paid vacations, or pensions. After opening my post on many mornings, I indulge in a few minutes of anguish and muted screams, then devote the next hour or more, if necessary, to tackling the mess. When I have satisfied myself that I have done the best I can by letter and telephone, I stand up from my desk and try to pretend I am not me, that I have no problems, that the past hour or more has not really happened, because I have to think myself into a state of innocence and the absence of worries of any kind in order to work. I suppose it's a measure of how professional one is, how quickly one can do this. The ability does improve with practice.

But at times I am so tense and tired after dealing with red tape, I feel like taking a nap for fifteen minutes. A nap clears the head wonderfully, besides giving fresh energy. I realize that about half the people in the world cannot nap without feeling logy afterward, but for those who can, a nap is a time-saver, not a time-waster. In my twenties, I had to do my own writing in the evenings, as my days were taken up with jobs or hack work. I got into the habit of napping around six, or of being able to if I wished, and of bathing and changing my clothes. This gave me an illusion of two days in one and made me as fresh for the evening, under the circumstances, as I could possibly be. Problems in writing can come unknotted in a miraculous way after a nap. I go to sleep with the problem, and wake up with the answer.

# CHAPTER 5

## ✎ PLOTTING

PLOTTING and *development* sound like processes that overlap, and they do to some extent. One cannot advance the development of a piece of fiction without getting some form of action, which is part of a plot. But the plotting I shall discuss here has to do with outlining and its ramifications, the work that comes after the idea has been developed, its elements decided.

For instance, where should one place the climax in a book? I am not sure every book has a special event that could be called a climax. Some plots will have an obvious climax, a surprise or something *bouleversant*. If this is so, then it is well to decide whether it should come in the middle, at the end, or three-quarters through a book. Some books may have two or three climaxes of equal importance. Some climaxes should be the last thing in a book, because after them, there is nothing to be said, and the book should end there, with a bang.

### Telling points

I think it is extremely good for a beginning writer to make an outline chapter by chapter—though the jottings for each chapter may be brief—because young writers are much inclined to ramble. The starting point for a chapter outline should be the question to oneself: "How will this chapter advance the story?" If you have a rambling, atmospheric, purple prose idea in mind for that chapter, be very wary; you may be wise to discard it, if it cannot be made to carry a point or two. But if you feel that your idea for a chapter will advance the story, then you should list the points you want to make in that chapter. Sometimes it is only one point: that a character is going blind and wants to conceal the fact; that a crucial letter has been stolen. Sometimes there are three points. And listing the points on a piece of scrap paper beside the typewriter will help make sure you are not going to neglect a point. I sometimes write points down even now, after writing fourteen books. I could have saved myself a good deal of work on my first book, *Strangers on a Train,* if I had done this from the start. There is no harm in doing it always, no matter how expert a writer becomes, as it gives him a rather solid feeling about the work ahead.

The temperament and character of the writer are reflected in his method of plotting: logical, illogical, pedestrian, inspired, imitative, original. A writer can be assured of a good living by imitating current trends and by being logical and pedestrian, because such imitations sell and do not take too much out of a writer in an emotional sense. Consequently, his production can be twice or ten times that of a more original writer who not only puts his back and his heart into his writing, but runs the risk of having the book rejected. It is well to try to assess yourself before starting to write. Since you can do this alone and in silence, there is no need for false pride.

I make this remark here, because it pertains to plotting. The public by and large is not fond of criminals who go free at the end, though they are more acceptable in books than in television and movie adaptations. Even though censorship has eased, a book is altogether more eligible for television and movie sales if the hero-criminal is caught, punished, and made to feel awful at the end. It is almost preferable to kill him in the course of the story, if the law is not going to. This goes against my grain, as I rather like criminals and find them extremely interesting, unless they are monotonously and stupidly brutal.

Criminals are dramatically interesting, because for a time at least they are active, free in spirit, and they do not knuckle down to anyone. I am so law-abiding, I can tremble before a customs inspector with nothing contraband in my suitcases. Perhaps I have some severe and severely repressed criminal drive in myself, or I would not take such an interest in criminals or write about them so often. And I think many suspense writers—except perhaps those whose heroes and heroines are the wronged and victimized parties, and whose villains are off-scene, unattractive or doomed—must have some kind of sympathy and identification with criminals, or they would not become emotionally engrossed in books about them. The suspense book is vastly different from the mystery story in this respect. The suspense writer often deals much more closely with the criminal mind, because the criminal is usually known throughout the book, and the writer has to describe what is going on in his head. Unless a writer is sympathetic, he cannot do this.

I find the public passion for justice quite boring and artificial, for neither life nor nature cares if justice is ever done or not. The public wants to see the law triumph, or at least the general public does, though at the same time the public likes brutality. The brutality must be on the right side, however. Sleuth-heroes can be brutal, sexually unscrupulous, kickers of women, and still be popular heroes, because they are chasing something worse than themselves, presumably.

### The almost incredible

I am very fond of coincidences in plots and situations that are almost but not quite incredible, as in the audacious plan set forth in the first chapter of *Strangers on a Train* by one man who has known the other passenger only a couple of hours; the chance selection of Tom Ripley, potential murderer, by the father of a young man, as an agent to bring that young man home from Europe; the unlikely and unpromising meeting of Robert and Jennie in *The Cry of the Owl*, when Robert appears to be a prowler and Jennie ignores this fact and is drawn to him. I am inclined to write books with slow, even tranquil beginnings, in which the reader becomes thoroughly acquainted with the hero-criminal and the people around him. But there is no law about this, and in *The Blunderer* I started out with a sharp bang, a brief chapter with considerable action—Kimmel's murder of his wife. We do not know much about Kimmel, still less about his wife, but it is an interesting first chapter because of the events. I then switched to Walter, the blunderer himself, and his part of the story begins very slowly indeed. We learn all about him, his unhappy relationship with his wife, his attraction to a girl named Ellie, more because her good nature is in contrast to his wife's ill-temper than for any other qualities about her.

### Tempo

It is part of the plotting, and of the effect one intends to make, this decision about tempo. I do not always think about it, as I did in *The Blunderer*. Partly it can be called "style," and as such is natural and unstudied, and has to do with the temperament of the writer. A very fast or slow tempo should not be attempted, if one feels strained and unnatural writing in it. Some books are nervous from the start, some slow all the way through, underplaying, analyzing and elaborating on the events. Some start slowly, pick up speed, and rush to the end. Can you imagine a suspense story by Proust? I can. The prose would be leisurely and involved, the action not necessarily so, and the motivations analyzed thoroughly.

Most of my slow, even tedious beginnings are written in a rather nervous prose. It is possible to describe a dull, sleepy villa on a sunny foreign beach in a febrile manner, though nothing happens for eighty pages. The prose style prepares the reader for violent things to come. More amusing, perhaps, would be to write in a leisurely manner (if it comes naturally), not preparing the reader at all for bloodshed and murder. It is absurd to try to make laws about these things. A writer should arrange the events in his story in the most amusing and entertaining sequence, and the right tempo of the prose, slow, fast or medium, will probably come of itself.

## Surprising yourself and your reader

I spoke earlier about the necessity of seeing a book as clearly as one sees a photograph, but I am almost never able to do this in the sense of seeing the whole *plot* as clearly as a photograph. I see my characters and the setting, the atmosphere, and what happens in the first third or quarter of a book, let's say, and usually the last quarter, but there is apt to be a foggy spot three-quarters of the way through, which I cannot clear up until I get there.

My methods of writing might drive a more logical person mad. But it often happens—even with writers who have seen their books clearly from start to finish before they begin—that a book changes itself three-quarters of the way through. This can be the result of a character's not behaving the way you foresaw, a situation that can be good or bad. I do not subscribe to the belief that having a vigorous character who acts for himself is always good. After all, you are the boss, and you don't want your characters running around all over the place, or possibly standing still, no matter how strong they may be.

A recalcitrant character may veer the plot in a better direction than you had thought of at the outset. Or he or she may have to be curbed, changed, or scrapped and rewritten entirely. Such a snag is worth a few days' pondering, and usually requires it. If the character is very stubborn and also interesting, you may have a different book from the one you set out to write, maybe a better book, maybe one just as good, but different. You should not be thrown by this experience. It happens quite often. And no book, and possibly no painting, when it is finished, is ever exactly like the first dream of it.

In case of a fuzzy spot in one's thinking—or in the manuscript—an obvious solution is apt to present itself. The obvious is the easy way out, usually not the best way. An obvious solution came to me when I was nearing the end of *The Story-Teller*: Sydney pushes his wife over a cliff on the estate of her parents in Kent, because she threatens to accuse him of trying to murder her (by pushing her over the cliff) if he does not stay married to her, which he does not care to do. So Sydney pushes her and tells a lie about her throwing herself over. This was a trite and obvious solution, which introduced Sydney's ability to murder too abruptly. I destroyed this version after writing it.

It is a cheap trick merely to surprise and shock the reader, especially at the expense of logic. And a lack of invention on the writer's part cannot be covered up by sensational action and clever prose. It is also a kind of laziness to write the obvious, which does not entertain, really. The ideal is an unexpected turn of events, reasonably consistent with the characters of the protagonists. Stretch the reader's credulity, his sense of logic, to the utmost—it is quite elastic—but don't break it. In this way, you will write something new, surprising and entertaining both to yourself and the reader.

# CHAPTER 6

## ✒ THE FIRST DRAFT

BEFORE we talk about the first draft, I would like to talk about the first page. It is important, because either it leads the reader into the story or it makes him close the book and put it aside. A writer I know told me he did not mind spending ten days on a first page. I would be blind on it in ten days, but I have done three versions in one day, and if I am still discontent, I go on to page two with an idea of looking at the first page again the next day. There is nothing like a fresh eye.

### First page

Some writers, assuming that a reader does not like to have his eye or brain taxed by a paragraph of thirty lines, prefer a short first paragraph of anywhere from one line to six. I think there is something in this. Thomas Mann can write a very long solid paragraph at the beginning of *Death in Venice*, for instance, but not everyone can write prose as intellectually fascinating as his.

I prefer a first sentence in which something moves

and gives action, rather than a sentence like: "The moonlight lay still and liquid on the pale beach."

Below are some of my first sentences, often more stewed over than they appear to be.

*Strangers on a Train*:

> The train tore along with an angry, irregular rhythm. It was having to stop at smaller and more frequent stations, where it would wait impatiently for a moment, then attack the prairie again.

This paragraph continues for a total length of seven lines and is followed by a two-line paragraph introducing the main character, Guy, who is in as restless a mood as the train:

> Guy took his eyes from the window and hitched himself back against the seat.

The next paragraph of three lines states a simple and familiar situation: Guy wants a divorce and is afraid his wife Miriam is going to make it difficult for him to get it. Then back to the train scene with Guy, in two medium-sized paragraphs which describe Guy's physical appearance, tell a little more about his problems, but do not strain the brain.

*The Talented Mr. Ripley*:

> Tom glanced behind him and saw the man coming out of the Green Cage, heading his way. Tom walked faster. There was no doubt the man was after him. Tom had noticed him five minutes ago, eyeing him carefully from a table as if he weren't *quite* sure, but almost. He

had looked sure enough for Tom to down his drink in a hurry, pay and get out.

This is followed by five or six short paragraphs of varying lengths, and by the bottom of the first page we know that Tom Ripley thinks he is in danger of being arrested, though we don't know for what.

*This Sweet Sickness*:

It was jealousy that kept David from sleeping, drove him from a tousled bed out of the dark and silent boarding house to walk the streets.

This sentence forms the whole first paragraph and is followed by a paragraph of eight lines, then one of seventeen lines—a rather "classic" first page. We don't learn anything about David's trouble, except that he is oppressed by something he calls the "Situation." Most of the page is devoted to describing the gloomy streets of the small upstate New York town in which he is walking, and David's melancholic view of the scene.

*The Glass Cell*:

It was 3:35 P.M., Tuesday afternoon, in the State Penitentiary, and the inmates were returning from the workshops.

This decidedly quiet sentence begins a paragraph of eighteen lines, followed by one twice as long. No doubt I was counting on the reader's curiosity about the unusual setting, a prison, to carry him along. The dreariness of the rhythm is the dreariness of the prison atmosphere also; a permeating hopelessness in Carter, at least at that moment, brought on by a disappointment he has just learned of, does not permit action, speed, or even nervousness. The first paragraph describes Carter's reaction to the everyday sounds of hundreds of men walking through stone corridors, and his reactions are those of an ordinary person, unused to prison life—the kind of person one may assume the majority of readers to be. At any rate, the reader is introduced to the prison scene through feelings and thoughts that might be his own in such circumstances, and he is not confused or taxed by any information as to what put Carter there. This can come later, after the reader is interested in Carter.

*The Blunderer*:

> The man in dark blue slacks and a forest green sport shirt waited impatiently in the line.

This forms the whole first paragraph. The second paragraph has nine lines, followed by one exchange of one-line casual conversation between the man and the girl selling movie tickets, then a paragraph of seven lines. The first sentence is not striking, but would be even less so without the word "impatiently." He is only going to a movie. Why should he be impatient? What's on his mind? In less than thirty lines, the reader learns, through action and not by my stating it, that the man has bought a ticket for the movie and greeted his friends there only to try to establish an alibi. In less than fifty lines, he is out of the movie house and on the way to do a murder. This is entertaining movement. We can find out more about Kimmel later, and we certainly do, but it is interesting at the start to see him in action.

In the first sentence of *This Sweet Sickness*, I meant to give a mood of emotional tension, of stubborn plodding also, of a bottling up of force that will one day explode. If a person is so upset that he will get out of bed to take a lonely walk, he is in some kind of trouble, and that is a "Situation."

There are no rules that I know of about all this, and I imagine one could have a character doing something both simple and interesting—like trying to fish a wedding ring out of a washbasin drain—and carry on for fifty or sixty lines in one paragraph and still hold the reader. But the reader does not want to be all at once plunged into a sea of information, complex facts to which he can scarcely relate any persons mentioned, because he has had no chance to meet them. Also, to fling the reader into an emotional scene, an argument, a scene of passion of any kind is a waste of fire, as the reader cannot possibly become involved in it without knowing the people involved. So I should say it is well to give a sense of movement without presenting all at once the reasons for the movement. In *Ripley*, "There was no doubt the man was after him." That is all we know, but it is a situation, and a simple, primitive one. But Ripley is thinking this. We do not know if Ripley is a crook who ought to be followed, if he is paranoid and is imagining it, but one man following another, or a man who thinks he is being followed, is a situation, and the reader wants to know if the "follower" is going to catch up with him, wants to catch up with him, and if so, what will happen.

Julian Symons is a first-class writer, a winner of many prizes for his suspense and mystery books, and a frequent contributor to *Ellery Queen's Mystery Magazine*. It would profit any mystery or suspense writer to study him. The first sentence of his book, *The Progress of a Crime* is:

Hugh Bennett had lunch that day as usual in Giuseppe's, which was the only good place to eat near the office.

The paragraph goes on for five lines, then there is casual conversation in paragraphs of increasing length which introduce us to two people who work with Hugh on an English small town newspaper. This is casual, unexciting prose which is still compelling reading simply because of its everydayness—except that they are talking shop. Newspaper shoptalk is interesting to most people, and in this case, the characters are griping, which is even more in eresting. *The Progress of a Crime* tells of young Hugh Bennett's coverage of a small town fracas on Guy Fawkes Day, during which a rather important man of the town is assaulted and stabbed to death by a gang of five adolescents. A trial of two of the gang follows, and its build-up, with newspaper publicity, is brilliantly described by Mr. Symons. There is essentially no mystery here, as we know the leader of the gang and one other boy must have wielded the knives involved. But there is suspense in the fighting between prosecution and defense to gather or to suppress evidence.

Julian Symons, an essayist and critic as well as a

novelist, is not hampered by categories, and his suspense novels illustrate the scope possible to this genre.

Graham Greene's celebrated *The Third Man* begins in a calm, narrative way:

> One never knows when the blow may fall. When I saw Rollo Martins first I made this note on him for my police files: "In normal circumstances a cheerful fool. Drinks too much and may cause a little trouble. Whenever a woman passes raises his eyes and makes some comment, but I get the impression that he'd really rather not be bothered. Has never really grown up and perhaps that accounts for the way he worshipped Lime." I wrote that phrase "in normal circumstances" because I met him first at Harry Lime's funeral.

There follows a longish paragraph ending with, "If only he had come to tell me then, what a lot of trouble would have been saved." Here, a mystery, a question, and a dead character are introduced in a paragraph that takes nearly the whole page, followed by an even longer paragraph of a page and a half, the two paragraphs forming the entire first chapter. The chapter has solidity, plus an engaging informality, and its facts are interspersed with human weakness—itself engaging, since we all have weaknesses and like to read about other people who have them, too. This was written for the films, and in a preface to *The Third Man*, Mr. Greene tells about his feeling of constraint, therefore.

Graham Greene's story, "The Basement Room" (published in 1935), on which the film, *The Fallen Idol*, was based, was not originally written for the films, and I think Mr. Greene is more at home and less self-conscious in its opening:

> When the front door had shut them out and the butler Baines had turned back into the dark heavy hall, Philip began to live. He stood in front of the nursery door, listening until he heard the engine of the taxi die out along the street. His parents were gone for a fortnight's holiday. . . .

And so on for four lines, then a paragraph of five lines, then eight, then six.

The difference in style between these two first pages is striking. I do not speak of their respective literary merit, but of mood. What hostility and self-defense are contained in the phrase "shut them out," instead of, for instance, simply "closed behind them." "The Basement Room" is in the tradition of the lyrical short story, seen through the eyes of one person (in this case a small boy) whose emotions are from the start involved. *The Third Man* is more intellectual. Mr. Greene is trying, as all writers try, to engage his readers, but in *The Third Man,* the trying seems more apparent. In the other, it is more natural.

A comment about first chapters in general: It is a good idea to provide lines of action in the first chapter. It may be that nothing "happens" in the first chapter; it may be that kind of story. You may want to set the scene, show the structure or pattern of relationship between two or more of the characters, introduce certain characters—and nothing more. By lines of action, I mean lines of potential action, such as:

the desire of one character to make a trip somewhere; of another to quit the scene and his inability to do so; the desire of a character for something (or someone) he or she does not yet have; or the mention of a potential danger—which can come from anything from termites and a possible earthquake to a mental aberration in one of the characters. Thus, merely to describe characters' relationships can create "a line of action," provided that the relationship is dynamic.

I can also imagine a quiet line of action: a beautiful young girl is faithfully tending her grandfather who is in a wheelchair, and is shutting out the world because of him. This really can't go on forever—not if you're writing a book about it! In the book, she may come out of the wheelchair world for a while, then go back to it at the end of the book—but if it is a suspense book, very likely she stays out. There should be either action or the promise of action in the first chapter of a suspense book. There is action or the promise of it in every good novel, but in suspense stories, the action is apt to be of a more violent kind. That is the only difference.

### Length and proportion

There are some writers who in their first drafts write too briefly. I have met one. But for that one, there are a hundred who will write too much. There is a tendency to overdescribe and even overexplain. In describing a room, for instance, it is not necessary to describe everything in it—unless the room is full of interesting incongruities like spider webs and wedding cakes. Usually, one thing, or two, will suffice to depict a room as rich, poor, neat, careless, fussy, masculine or feminine.

In dialogue, too, the tyro is inclined to set every word down. It is often possible to give the gist of a conversation of forty lines in three lines of prose. Dialogue is dramatic and should be used sparingly, because the effect will be more dramatic when it is used. For example, a marital wrangle in a book may be summed up: "Howard refused to budge, though she argued with him for a full half hour. At last she gave up." One might after this add a single speech with a paragraph to itself, such as, "You've always had your way," Jane said. "So chalk up one more victory."

In writing a first draft, the book as a whole should be kept in mind, that is to say, in proportion—whether one sees every part of it in detail from start to finish or not. I can best illustrate what I mean by describing my first attempt at writing a book, which was also my first failure. The book was never published and never even finished. I could see the whole book at that time—beginning, middle and end. I meant it to be some three hundred pages long, and after arriving at this, I intended to cut twenty-five or so. One day I found myself on page three hundred and sixty-five, and not quite half my story had been told. I had kept my nose so diligently to the page, I could no longer see the book as a whole. I was writing elaborately about small matters, and the book was no longer in proportion.

If we pretend the book is a domino-shape, without white dots but with a ridge down the middle, then let the ridge stand for the middle of the story—so far as the number of pages goes, and as the length of plot goes. Minor climaxes and events might be on either side of the central line, but not all crowded in just after the central line, and not all at the extreme right end of the domino. A concept like this may help to keep a book under control. Of course, there is room for some variation in what you have decided ought to be "the middle," and a slight variation is not serious, but should you be seventy-five pages off the mark one way or the other, something is wrong.

Some writers may prefer an easily seen diagram as an outline, or in addition to a written outline. I once made one which looked like a graph line going up, down, up, down. The *up* points were labeled with certain events of the story. This method forces a writer to see the sequence of events in proportion to the entire story. He could also label the points tentatively with page numbers—which would show at least roughly where he ought to be in pages by the time he is at a particular point in the story.

I make it a habit to think about the next day's work at the end of a day's stint. Possibly I am a bit tired and glad the eight-page section, or whatever, is done. But it is pleasant and encouraging to think of the next events in the story, the events I shall write about tomorrow. It gives me a sense of continuity. If I am going to be distracted by friends that evening, I do not feel so far away from the work (dangerously so, I mean), even if I don't think about work the entire evening. In fact, it's a good idea not to think about it, but to let the mind recreate itself in the evening among friends, or by doing something quite different from writing. If you think about the next day's work at the end of a day, you go to the typewriter the next morning with a rather definite job to do, instead of the vague feeling of "Where was I? How am I going to get back into *this*?" It also helps to sleep on ideas; you will write them more quickly and clearly the next day.

A book is really a long continuous process, which, ideally, should be interrupted only by sleep. Since we do not live on desert islands, and even a cabin in the woods would present problems like seeing about food and fuel supply, we must constantly be scheming and playing games and inventing crutches of one kind or another. Certainly the mind needs recreation while you are writing a book, but it should be of a carefully chosen kind, not a disturbing or physically tiring kind.

I seldom read over the whole of the previous day's work before starting to work, but I read the last page or two I have written. If on the previous day I did not stop at the end of a chapter, I check to see how long the chapter already is, as I like to be aware of chapter length—even though there are no laws about chapter length. A chapter is like a little "act" in a play, and has a dramatic or emotional bang in it, whether small or big. One must be emotionally aware of this. I have been asked often about this little matter—whether I read the preceding day's work (or even the whole manuscript, as I think Hemingway did) before starting to work each day—and so I mention it here. It is a purely individual matter, whether or how much one reads back. I find it necessary to read at least a page back in order to resume the pace of the prose and its mood.

### Mood and pace

I began *The Talented Mr. Ripley* in what I thought was a splendid mood, a perfect pace. I had taken a cottage in Massachusetts in the country near Lenox, and I spent the first three weeks there reading books from the excellent privately maintained library in Lenox, which, however, welcomes tourist patronage. I read an 1835 edition of de Tocqueville's *Democracy in America* and browsed in an Italian grammar, among other things. My landlord, who lived not far away, was an undertaker, very voluble about his profession, though he drew the line at permitting me to visit his establishment and see the tree-shaped incision he made in the chest before stuffing the corpse. "What do you stuff the corpse with?" I asked. "Sawdust," he replied bluntly and matter of factly. I was toying with the idea of having Ripley engaged in a smuggling operation that involved a train ride from Trieste to Rome and Naples, during which Ripley would escort a corpse that was actually filled with opium. This was certainly a wrong tack, and I never wrote it that way, but this was why I was interested in seeing my landlord's corpses. In my bucolic mood, I started the book, and it seemed to be going along very well. But on page seventy-five or so, I began to feel that my prose was as relaxed as I was, very nearly flaccid, and that a relaxed mood was not the one for Mr. Ripley. I decided to scrap the pages and begin again, mentally as well as physically sitting on the edge of my chair, because that is the kind of young man Ripley is—a young man on the edge of his chair, if he is sitting down at all.

But during these meanderings of opium-filled corpses and the mistake of leisurely prose, I did not turn loose of my main idea, which was of two young men with a certain resemblance—not much—one of whom kills the other and assumes his identity. This was the crux of the story. Many stories can be written around such an idea. There is nothing spectacular about the plot of *Ripley*, I think, but it became a popular book because of its frenetic prose, and the insolence and audacity of Ripley himself. By thinking myself inside the skin of such a character, my own prose became more self-assured than it logically should have been. It became more entertaining. A reader likes to feel that the writer is quite in command of his material and has strength to spare. *Ripley* won an award from the Mystery Writers of America, and the Grand Prix de Littérature Policière in France, and was made into the movie *Purple Noon*. The Mystery Writers of America award hangs in my bathroom, where I hang awards, as they look less pompous there. In Positano, the framed and glassed-in document became slightly mildewed, and when I removed the glass to clean and dry it, I lettered "Mr. Ripley and" before my own name, since I think Ripley himself should have received the award. No book was easier for me to write, and I often had the feeling Ripley was writing it and I was merely typing.

**In tune with the book**

Good books write themselves, and this can be said from a small but successful book like *Ripley* to longer and greater works of literature. If the writer thinks about his material long enough, until it becomes a part of his mind and his life, and he goes to bed and wakes up thinking about it—then at last when he starts to work, it will flow out as if by itself. A writer should feel geared to his book during the time he is writing it, whether that takes six weeks, six months, a year or more. It is wonderful the way bits of information, faces, names, anecdotes, all kinds of impressions that come in from the outside world during the writing period, will be usable in the book, if one is in tune with the book and its needs. Is the writer attracting the right things, or is some process keeping out the wrong ones? Probably it's a mixture of both.

If you are trying to write while holding a job, it is important for you to have a certain length of time every day or every weekend which is sacred, and during which there are no interruptions. In a way, this is easier to arrange if you live with someone, because that person can answer a doorbell or a telephone. There must be hundreds of writers who are trying to write a novel on weekends and in the evenings. Five evenings a week of two or three hours' work each evening, or every Saturday for eight hours, or four evenings per week of three hours—a writer must make his own schedule and stick to it. A sense of pride in your work is essential, and if you permit interruptions and accept invitations, your pride is slowly tarnished. The progress on a novel may be slow, but that is not important. The important thing is to have the feeling the book is on the rails, going fine as far as it has gone—even if you've done only forty pages after a month. If you have a job, you should be fresh for post-job stints and should not try to rush, as things then get into a tangle. Tangles are not easy to face, so if a distraction presents itself, you are more inclined to yield to it than to face the problem waiting on your desk.

## Craft and talent

These remarks are platitudinous, yet writers of some experience and certainly of some talent must suffer from external pressures, or there would be no institution like Yaddo at Saratoga Springs. Yaddo costs no money to go to, but a writer must present a first chapter of a book, a few short stories, published or not, and have three recommendations to be admitted. Here nothing is provided for the writer but a room to himself and a guarantee that there will be no interruptions from 9 A.M. until 4 P.M., but a writer doesn't need anything else except a pencil or a typewriter and some paper—and food, of course, which is gratis, too. Most writers find that they work thirty percent better under such conditions than they do "out in the world," wherever that may be for them. Their writing is better, and their production is faster. Not everyone is lucky enough to go to Yaddo, because of the necessity of holding a job. I mention it as an ideal, something one can aim at in small measures even in a household with wife and children.

One need not be a monster, or feel like one, to demand two or three hours' absolute privacy here and there. This schedule should become a habit, and the habit, like writing itself, a way of life. It should become a necessity; then one can and will always work. It is possible to think like a writer all one's life, to want to be a writer, yet to write seldom, out of laziness or lack of habit. Such a person may write passably well when he writes—such people are known as great letter writers—and may even sell a few things, but that is doubtful. Writing is a craft and needs constant practice.

"Painting is not a matter of dreaming, or being inspired. It is a handicraft, and a good craftsman is needed to do it well." Pierre Auguste Renoir said that, and that from an artist and a master I think is worth remembering.

And from Martha Graham on the art of dancing: "It's a curious combination of skill, intuition, and I must say ruthlessness—and a beautiful intangible called faith. If you don't have this magic, you can do a beautiful thing, you can do thirty-two fouettés, and it doesn't matter. This thing, I guess it's born in you. It's a thing you can draw out in people, but you cannot instill it in people, you cannot teach it."

Renoir speaks of the craft, Martha Graham of the talent, flair, genius. The two must go together. Craft without talent has no joy and no surprises, nothing original.

Talent without craft—well, how can the world ever see it?

Great musicians and sculptors and actors have made remarks similar to those above, for all the arts are one, all artists have a core and a similar one, and it is just an accident that determines whether an artist becomes musician, painter, or writer. All art is based on a desire to communicate, a love of beauty, a need to create order out of disorder. This was my "Eureka!" at seventeen, that all the arts were one. I felt it, and I actually thought I had discovered something new, but I soon found it had been said thousands of years before, almost as long ago as man was writing anything. And twenty and forty thousand years ago, when the great animal murals of the Lascaux Caves were being painted, I imagine some man or two in the tribe remarked a curious similarity of temperament between the men painting bison and reindeer on the cave walls and the men who were always telling stories they had made up, always trying to get a group around them to listen. The efforts of the storyteller to perfect his art are unrecorded, but the floors of the decorated caves are strewn with the first efforts, the practice sketches of the wall-painters, on fragments of now broken clay. They had to practice before they could draw a reindeer's back with one sweep of hand and arm.

### A sense of contact

I wonder at certain painters I have heard about, but never met, who are content to paint for themselves, not caring if they ever have a show, much less sell a picture. This requires self-sufficiency indeed. All pleasure for them apparently comes from perfecting their work before their own eyes, for themselves alone. This seems strange, as long as there are people around them, and perhaps some of them do have a select group of friends to whom they like to show their work. But such an attitude is not impossible to imagine. I think the majority of writers, living a Robinson Crusoe existence with no hope of seeing another human being as long as they lived, would still write poems, short stories and books with whatever material there was at hand. Writing is a way of organizing experience and life itself, and the need of this is still present though an audience may not be. However, I think most painters and writers like to think of their work being seen and read by lots of people, and emotionally this sense of contact is of great importance to their morale.

I think my first push in the direction of writing came when I was nine years old. My English teacher gave a typically painful assignment, a composition on the subject of "How I Spent My Summer Vacation." This was made more excruciating by the fact we had to recite it without notes, standing at the front of the class. Usually, our compositions of this nature were about bicycle outings, roller skate races, or how someone made a slingshot and won second prize in a contest of hitting tin cans. But the summer I was nine I had done something interesting. My family had driven from New York to Texas and back, and en route we had visited the Endless Caverns. I described these caves, which had made a tremendous impression on me—because of their size, the fact the end of the caverns had not yet been found, and the flowerlike shapes that some of the limestone took, making flowers with stamens, anthers, petals and stems. The caverns had been discovered by two small boys who were chasing a rabbit. The rabbit dashed down a crevice in the earth, the boys followed it, and found themselves in an underground world—huge, cool, beautiful and full of color. When I came to this part, there was a different atmosphere in the classroom. Everyone had begun to listen, because they were interested. I had suddenly become entertaining, and I was also sharing a personal emotion. I forgot my self-consciousness, and my little speech went much better. This was my first experience at giving enjoyment through a story. It was like a kind of magic, yet it could be done and had been done by me. I did not think these thoughts at the time, however, and I was fifteen before I tried to write anything for my own pleasure, and then it was a fantastic romantic epic poem, something like one of Tennyson's *Idylls of the King.*

# CHAPTER 7

## ❧ THE SNAGS

IT IS perhaps ridiculous to call a chapter "snags" and attempt to list them and deal with them in a few pages. There are potential snags everywhere, even in the first sentence, if one writes a dull one, becomes dissatisfied, and pauses. Snags cause pauses of various kinds and various lengths. Small snags, like a dull sentence, can be corrected in two minutes by writing the sentence over, but there are big snags which might be described as writing oneself into a corner. The big ones occur in the last half of books and may cause agonized pauses of days and weeks. One feels trapped, hands tied, brain tied, characters paralyzed, the story dying before it is finished. The cure for this may be to go back to the original idea, back to your thoughts in the time before you began to write the book. Remind yourself of what impelled you to start the book. Even ask yourself, "What do I want to happen?" and then arrange things so that it can happen. This may mean changing the plot or a character a little—or a lot. And of course this is the longest of operations. Sometimes, if you are stuck merely for an incident, an event to wind the book up, clear the hero, or whatever, the operation is shorter.

In writing *Ripley*, I did have a snag some twenty pages before the end. I wanted an incident which would appear to be perilous for Ripley, but which would clear him in the eyes of the police. The idea simply wouldn't come, and wouldn't for nearly three weeks. I began to feel that my power of invention had deserted me. I tried every method I knew, thinking about it, not thinking about it, reading the preceding fifty pages, but nothing worked. Since I felt I was wasting time, I began typing up the first part in final form with carbons. This semi-mechanical activity, which was at the same time concerned with the book (I was of course polishing as I went), must have done the trick, because the solution came to me when I had been typing for three or four days. It was to have the string come untied on the oil paintings done by Greenleaf and signed by him, in the storage room of the American Express, Venice, where Ripley has left them. The fingerprints on these paintings are presumed to be Greenleaf's, because he is supposed to have left the paintings in Venice before his "suicide." Greenleaf had actually been dead for months before this. The fingerprints on the paintings match those in "Greenleaf's" apartment in Rome, which Ripley is not suspected of having been in, and from a police point of view, this checks, though the fingerprints are all Ripley's. Ripley is cleared, and to top it all, receives the blessings of Greenleaf's father, plus Greenleaf's income for life. End of story.

What a writer wants to have happen in a story is concerned with the effect he wants to create—tragedy, comedy, melancholy, or whatever. You should be aware of what effect you want to create before starting the book. I repeat this here, because it can be of help in case of a snag. Return again to the effect you intended, and the incident or change of plot may spring to mind at once.

As I write this book, I find myself bogged down in a series of annoying but predictable snags. They are small snags. What to say next? Doesn't this or that remark belong in a chapter past or a chapter to come? At moments, I feel I have a lot to say, and at other moments feel blank. This is because I am trying to use my brain instead of some unconscious force on the whole thing, and above all because this book has no thread of narrative to guide me through its small labyrinth. If this kind of snag were to occur in a work of fiction, I would know it was because I could not see the events immediately ahead (in which case, I would stop and get the next thirty or forty pages thought out), or because I was forcing some character or characters to do something against their grain, or because the plot was so illogical, it was not convincing even to me.

Careless as I may sound about plotting and writing, I do believe in seeing ahead one chapter beyond the chapter I am writing, and this is more than a day's work in the writing usually. There are some beginning writers who can go romping on and fill two hundred pages in no time, but much of the time, an editor does the work for him, pointing out inconsistencies and actions out of character. It is both lazy and insensitive for a writer to write like this. A writer should always be sensitive to the effect he is creating on paper, to the verisimilitude of what he is writing. He should sense when something is wrong, as quickly as a mechanic hears a wrong noise in an engine, and he should correct it before it becomes worse.

## Abstract and concrete problems

If a suspense story is laid out as logically as possible, then the writing should go along more easily than the writing of a straight novel, because of a strong story line. Straight novelists have rather abstract problems—a character who refuses to bend to the writer's plot, a solution to a moral problem which seemed right in outline but is not right when set down in prose. A suspense writer's problems are often concrete and have to do with things like the speed of a train, police procedure, the fatality of sleeping pills, limits of physical strength, and the reasonable boundary of police stupidity or intelligence. Geography may have to be changed, distances shortened or lengthened. The hero may have to be given a special talent or handicap, such as sharp eyesight or hearing, a morbid fear of moths or butterflies, and this will have to be planted very early in the book, if one intends to make use of it later.

The beginning writer's most frequent snag may take the form of the question, "What happens next?" This is a terrifying question, which can leave the writer shaking with stage fright, and, moreover, with a feeling of standing naked on a stage in front of a lot of people without even an act to do to amuse them. He has been suddenly forced to think about something which surely

never came to him by thinking, for inspiration or the
germ of an idea never does. Quite often he knows two
or three things which ought to happen next or very
soon; he is not at all blank about his story, but he cannot decide which scene or event should be written next.
This is merely a problem of sequence, simple, as problems go. But it is a dramatic problem, therefore a creative one. If you cannot decide it by thought, then stop
thinking and do something else—like washing the car—
and let the three ideas ramble around freely in your
mind. The writer's mind has a way of arranging a chain
of events in a naturally dramatic, and therefore correct
form. From the greatest of dramatists—Aeschylus and
Shakespeare—down to successful hacks, this dramatic
arrangement of events is manifest in a way that is often
called instinctive, but is a product of practice and disci-
pline, too. Writers are entertainers. It delights them to
present things in an appealing, entertaining form, to
make the audience or the reader sit up with surprise
and take notice and enjoy themselves.

### Which point of view?

But if a story really refuses to move and there is a
sense of a motionless tangle, try going back to the methods of plotting: Invent possible solutions to your problem; invent action to carry the story on, even wild and
illogical solutions and actions, because perhaps they can
be made logical. If this fails, forget the whole thing for
a while, or even pretend you don't care whether the
book is ever finished or not. This may mean a few days

of wandering around the house doing nothing, or gardening, playing the piano or doing anything that changes your thoughts. The snag in a book is a lurking problem that has to be solved, however, and that fact cannot be swept away by pretending. Of course it can be very easily pushed aside, if you are not really involved in the book. But if you are involved and care, your unconscious will come up with the solution to the problem.

A writer may find on page twenty or so that he is telling his story from the wrong point of view. I think point of view is a bugaboo for many beginning writers, because so many terrifying things have been said about it. It is entirely a matter of feeling comfortable in the writing, the question of through whose eyes you should tell the story. The only other matter to think of is, what kind of story is it? Would it be better told from the sidelines, or through the eyes of a participant?

The first-person singular is the most difficult form in which to write a novel; on this writers seem to be agreed, even if they agree on no other matter in regard to point of view. I have bogged down twice in first-person-singular books, so emphatically that I abandoned any idea of writing the books. I don't know what was the matter, except that I got sick and tired of writing the pronoun "I", and I was plagued with an idiotic feeling that the person telling the story was sitting at a desk writing it. Fatal! Also, I have quite a bit of introspection in my heroes, and to write all this in the first person makes them sound like nasty schemers, which of course they are, but they seem less so if some all-knowing author is telling what is going on in their heads.

Perhaps because it is all round easier for me, I prefer the point of view of the main character, written in the third-person singular, and I might add masculine, as I have a feeling which I suppose is quite unfounded that women are not so active as men, and not so daring. I realize that their activities need not be physical ones and that as motivating forces they may well be ahead of the men, but I tend to think of women as being pushed by people and circumstances instead of pushing, and more apt to say, "I can't" than "I will" or "I'm going to."

The very easiest point of view, I hardly dare to remark, might be that of a non-criminal person in a story in which he or she is pitted against the criminal. Obviously, the writer must identify with the person through whose eyes the story is being told, for it is that person's feelings, thoughts, and reactions that will be the lifeblood of the story. This is not the same as saying that this character will be the *action* of the story. I can easily imagine a suspense story told through the eyes of an old man or woman confined to a sickbed, merely an observer of what goes on. But even a suspense novel is, like all novels, an emotional thing; it is the five senses, plus the intellect which judges and makes decisions, that count and form the real book.

Suspense novelists are apt to choose the point of view of an active person—a man able to fight, run, and use a gun, if need be. This can also become boring both to readers and to the writer, if constantly repeated. It has crossed my mind to write a suspense book from the corpse's point of view. "This is the corpse speaking." And then he or she proceeds to tell the story preceding his or her death, the details of dying, death, and then what is going on afterward. Never mind asking how a corpse can do all this. In fiction, it is not always necessary to answer logical questions. But I am hardly original in this idea. It has been used by more than half a dozen crime novelists, according to the late Anthony Boucher, and he adds, "It keeps recurring to people, always as a new and striking idea . . ."

We should not forget the bystander point of view, or the brilliant use of it made by Henry James in *The Turn of the Screw*, for instance. I can't imagine that governess holding her own in a pillowfight with the two children, but her reactions to the things she saw, or imagined, make one's hair stand on end. Charlotte Armstrong makes good use of a woman's or wife's point of view throughout stories in which horror lurks in a kitchen broom closet or scratches at the windowpanes of an ordinary house. This might be called evil-through-the-eyes-of-innocence, yet her characters are not bystanders, they are quite involved in the action.

I prefer two points of view in a novel, but I don't always have them. In *Deep Water*, I might have switched from Vic's, the husband's, point of view to the wife's, if I had wished to, but in the story we know so plainly what her rather primitive thoughts and desires are, it would have brought little information or variation to the book to see things through her eyes. Yet, keeping a single point of view throughout a book, as I did in *The Talented Mr. Ripley*, increases the intensity of a story—and intensity can and should offset a possible monotony of a one-person viewpoint. Using two points of view—as I did in *Strangers on a Train*, of the two young men protagonists who are so different, and in *The Blunderer*, Walter and Kimmel, again vastly different people—can bring a very entertaining change of pace and mood. This is why I prefer the two-person point of view, if the story can possibly take it.

Recently I read a story in a woman's magazine, a story seen through a father's eyes: His young daughter was in danger of being whisked away by an older man whom she thought fascinating. These stories usually start out: "I'm only a man, so I don't know everything, but . . ." Readers presumably read on avidly, just because the narrator is a man and is supposed to know things that they don't. The story went along all right for a thousand words or so; then there was a romantic scene between the daughter and the older man on a terrace in the moonlight, with direct dialogue, and the father could not possibly have been there. Nor did the author announce that he was going to invent the conversation, but I was halfway through this scene before the fact dawned on me. So it goes with popular fiction.

Why worry about point of view? You might as well have a spittoon in the corner talking next. Still, because I am a writer, the handling of the viewpoint in this story did finally jolt me, and I went back to see how the writer had managed it. He hadn't; he had simply started writing the scene on the moonlit terrace. The result is readable—especially if you have to interrupt the story to stir a bowl of soup—but emotionally speaking, the break, the inexplicable, unforgivable break in point of view weakened the story. This was a bit more of a liberty than a writer can take—a horrible deformation of a short story, in fact. Of course, the terrace scene was written to sell the story, because most people want to see the two romantic protagonists in action and not read a father's analysis of it all. And it would have made us dislike the father if he had admitted frankly, "I am an eavesdropper, and I hid in a large vase on the terrace that night and . . ."

### "Feeling" a story emotionally

A serious bogging down after thirty or forty pages, a really sour feeling about the whole project, may come from the writer's not identifying with the person through whose eyes and emotions he is trying to tell the story. Experienced writers learn to recognize this at once, by page one or two, or can often sense it while they are thinking—that is, trying to feel the story emotionally—before starting to write. Only two months ago, I had such a problem with a short story about a woman of forty-five, a resident of Munich, who comes to an Austrian ski resort hotel with an idea of committing suicide in a few days. But far from being melancholic, she has a joy about her, a look of quiet happiness which makes her attractive to both men and women in the hotel, to young and to old. She has come to terms with herself, with the events of her life, and though she has always been fond of people, she no longer needs them—which is the theme of the story. This is why people are drawn to her, because they sense that she will take nothing from them, emotionally speaking.

Well, I made two beginnings on this, one of six pages and the other of twelve. Neither of them rang true. The prose seemed forced, self-conscious, utterly without life, and above all I wanted to convey a sense of life and of loving life, even in the woman who wished to leave it. I mentioned to a friend how disgusted I was with myself, because I could not write this story which had such a promising theme. I had depressing thoughts that the theme, even though I had thought of it, was better than I was as a writer. Henry James or Thomas Mann could easily write it, but not I. "I'm thinking of writing it from the point of view of someone at the hotel who observes her," I said, but this did not fill me with much hope. Then my friend, who is not a writer, suggested I try it from the omniscient author's point of view.

This, at least, was an idea. The word "omniscient" to me suggested an objectivity. The all-knowing author observes the whole thing as if from a distance. I tried the story again, thinking myself "at a distance," though in fact I still wrote through the eyes of my heroine. It was only the word "omniscient" that had helped. I no longer had to think I should be inside the main character, a woman on the very edge of suicide. I have never been on the edge of suicide or anywhere near it, and I have no doubt that this handicapped me. To imagine the renunciation of the world that suicide means would be a colossal task for me, and it would take a long time and a lot of effort to do it properly. So I took the easy way out and did not explain her state of mind. (Never apologize, never explain, said a French diplomat, and a French writer, Baudelaire, said that the only good parts of a book are the explanations that are left out.) I said only that her husband and son were alive, and were quite unlike her, and that consequently they had been estranged for some years.

On the other hand, I have never been on the verge of murdering anybody, and I can write about that all right, perhaps because murder is often an extension of anger, an extension to the point of insanity or temporary insanity.

The story of the woman who committed suicide is called "Nothing That Meets the Eye." It is always nice to be able to say that a story made the Hit Parade or was anthologized three times, but this one was never sold.

It is inevitable in a writer's first efforts that the choice of point of view will be governed by his personality, by what kind of life he has had, how and where he was brought up, the personal things. Obviously, it is wiser to choose first the point of view of characters who resemble oneself emotionally. With practice at imagining, one can dare step into other kinds of people—farmer, child, young girl, a sailor, or anything else one is not. Like Paul Gallico, one might finally even step into a cat.*

Many snags are somehow in the writer's mind rather

* In his book, *The Silent Miaow,* the personal confessions of a cat.

than on paper. He slows down, or stops, without quite realizing what the trouble is. Often he has a vague feeling of unsureness, that he is going off somewhere, that the story is no longer good or convincing. I had this feeling briefly while writing *The Story-Teller* when it came time for the wife, Alicia, to become so distraught that she flung herself over the cliff. The trouble was, I had not established early enough in the book that she was the kind of person who might break under a strain. She did finally fling herself over a cliff, but I had to make it logical in earlier pages that she could and might. This is a simple instance of such bogging down, but it is the kind that frequently turns up in one form or another: the writer has not laid the groundwork early for what he wants to do later in the story.

### Using the senses

A neglect of atmosphere is hardly a snag, but can give a writer a thin-ice feeling as he progresses, without his knowing why. I cannot think of a formula for creating atmosphere, but since atmosphere comes in through any or all of the five senses, or a sixth also, one should make use of them. How a house smells, the general color of a room—olive green, musty brown, or cheerful yellow. And sounds—that of a tin can being blown down a street, of an invalid coughing in another room, the mingled smell of medicaments, often dominated by camphor, that is in many old people's rooms. Or on a country estate where nothing seems wrong or threatening, one may feel for no reason that the trees are about to fall inward and demolish the house.

Years ago I visited some friends of friends in a two-story house near New Orleans. The house was very new, in fact the couple who lived there had just finished building it and had just been married, yet I remember feeling that the staircase, the living room, the hall above the staircase was haunted. I do not believe in ghosts, despite all the supporting stories there are, so my feeling was even odder. I did not mention it to anyone. It was a feeling not so much of a presence that might walk down those uncarpeted new pine stairs, but a sense of gloom and tragedy to come. I never saw or heard of the people again. It would be eerie indeed if they had both been killed in a car accident a few months later.

## Other professions

Writers should take every opportunity to learn about other people's professions, what their workrooms look like, what they talk about. Varying the professions of the story's characters is one of the hardest things for a writer to do after three or four books, when he has used up the few he knows about. Not many writers have the chance to learn about new lines of work, once they become full-time writers. In a small town, where everybody knows everybody, a writer might have an easier time of it. The carpenter might let him come out on some jobs with him. A lawyer friend may let him sit in his office sometimes and take notes. I once took a job during Christmas rush at a department store in Manhattan. Here was a scene chaotic with detail, sounds, people, and a new tempo—pretty hectic—an unending stream of little dramas that one could observe in customers, fellow workers and the management, which was full of self-importance. I made good use of this new scene in my writing. A writer should seize upon every new scene that comes his way, take notes, and turn it to account. It is the same for new towns, cities and countries. Or even new streets: A derelict street anywhere, full of ashcans, kids, stray dogs, is just as fertile for the imagination as a sunset at Sounion, where Byron carved his name in one of the marble columns of Apollo's temple.

# CHAPTER 8

## ❧ THE SECOND DRAFT

I USED to make a complete second draft, and then a
third, which I typed with two carbons, that was the final
draft. Lately, I am a little more efficient and do not
have to retype every page of my first draft to form a
second draft, but I still have that stage called "second
draft," when my corrected manuscript has no carbon.

The first thing to do in starting a second draft is to
read through the first, as if you were a reader who had
never seen the book before. You cannot quite achieve
this state, but try your best. It is just as well not to
twiddle about trying to improve on an adjective or a
verb, but to read on quickly to see the pace of the thing,
to feel where it lags, to see where it is unclear, where
there is a sort of emotional gap in one character's or
several characters' progress. Faults such as these, when
one finds them, strike one so forcibly—like a criticism
uttered out loud that makes one wince—that it is usually not necessary to make notes on them, but there is
no harm in doing so, provided the notes aren't too long
and do not keep one too long from the reading. Page

number jottings might be enough. If in this first reading any sentences seem unnecessary or redundant, strike them out at once, as it will only have to be done later. It doesn't take long to strike out a sentence with a crayon, and it gives one the proper cavalier attitude toward one's own prose, which should not be held sacred.

"A little more detail in flashback of picnic P. 66," is the kind of note that might be useful to make, as this is the kind of thing one might forget and also not notice on a second reading. Above all, one should find out the general impression the book makes in its present form. Is the hero too priggish, tough, humorless, selfish? Is he admirable, if you want him to be admirable? Does the reader care about him?

### Liking and caring

Be honest about the last question. It is not the same as liking the hero. It is caring whether he goes free, or caring that he is caught rightly at the end, and it is being interested in him, pro or con. It is skill that makes the reader care about characters. It must start with the writer caring. This is much of what that rather stuffy word "integrity" is about. Good hack writers may not care a damn, and yet through their skillful methods give an illusion that they do, and furthermore convince the reader that he cares, too. To care about a character, hero or villain, takes time and also a kind of affection, or better said, affection takes time and also knowledge, which takes time, and hack writers don't have it.

One should think now and then about the painter's

art. If a painter is doing a portrait, one he wants to be good, he will not just draw a hasty oval for the head and stick in two dots for the eyes and so forth. He will see how the sitter's eyes are different from other people's, and he will also take the trouble to choose five or six colors from his palette to paint the hair and the flesh— white, green, red, brown and yellow. A writer should use as much care in depicting the face and appearance of his main characters, but he should do it briefly (more difficult than doing it at length), as briefly as he can and still have the reader remember.

I'm aware that some writers are of a different opinion and couldn't care less what color hair their heroes have because it doesn't matter to them. If a man is of medium height with dark hair, that's enough for some. I am only saying how I prefer to write. In fact, I recently read a review highly praising a suspense book in which nothing was said about the characters' looks or about their backgrounds. What they were like was shown entirely through action. A few days later, I read another review of the same book, not praising it at all, but insisting that people *were* different, did have backgrounds, and that one couldn't write a good book leaving these facts out. Thus the little battle rages.

### Polish with profit

By the time I have read through the first draft of a manuscript, I may have a list of five spots to be taken care of—awkward writing, a section too brief, a point not emphasized enough—and a mental list of things like "terribly boring when he comes to visit old aunt." I assume that being boring in a section is such a dire fault, it will not be forgotten. Unless I am emotionally exhausted for the day—and reading one's own manuscript can be emotionally exhausting—then the biggest problem should be tackled first. When this is licked, I start feeling better. Big problems can sometimes take days to correct, however, especially if I have to come up with a fresh idea. There is bound to be considerable retyping in this period. If a page of mine finally gets full of changed words, added sentences and so forth, I retype it just for the sake of neatness. Even though I can still read it, I am probably the only person in the world who can, and that not easily.

I do not begrudge the time it takes to type over sloppy pages. I am creating my second draft as I go, and I am also constantly polishing, improving on a word as I type that I had not bothered improving when I corrected the first draft with a pen. A writer can polish with profit until the last moment before a manuscript goes to the publishing house. And if it is accepted, he can still polish with profit until it goes to the printer. Poets are always polishing—I have heard of some polishing the printed page—and they are the greatest carers of all about words.

Clarity should be in the front of your mind at all times. It is the best guide to a good style also. In a suspense book, it is vital. Fuzzy sentences should be clarified when you read the first draft, and if it takes too long to do this in the first reading, write "unclear" in the margin, so you will go back to it.

I often find I can profitably cut one or two sentences

at the end of a chapter, sentences which perhaps I strained to produce, because I thought the chapter needed them to be rounded off. An example of this is: "And so he walked disconsolately out of the house. He had learned what he came to find out." The reader should know he learned what he came to find out, if he has read the preceding chapter, and it can be assumed a character can walk out of a house or will walk out eventually, if he doesn't live there and has a home to go to.

If you have cut a great deal in one or two readings, you might want to renumber the pages, guessing approximately how much shorter each page is. This is important if you are aiming at a certain number of pages, because a certain publishing house wants that number —and no more. Publishers are shy of long books, because of production costs which can raise the retail price of the book and cut down sales. Other publishers cannot fit a short book into their pattern, so it is a good idea to aim at a definite length, if you want to submit to a paperback house, and possibly a different length for a hardcover house. Most writers prefer to express length in word-number: 60,000 words are two hundred and forty pages, for instance, since there are a thousand words in the average four typed pages, and a manuscript page is approximately the length of a printed page. If you are aiming at a certain market, it is best to have the length correct from the start. Doubleday, for example, happens to want books of two hundred and forty pages in length, while Harper & Row will take them a bit longer.

## CHAPTER 9

### ✖ THE REVISIONS

IN THE second draft, a writer makes all the changes and improvements he knows how to make, and the final typing has probably smoothed over a few more rough spots. These are revisions by definition, but the revisions I speak of are those asked by other people—the editors or sometimes an agent. If an editor remarks that something is unclear—even though it is something you have written over twice to make clear—then it is a good idea for you to try to make it clearer. If it is not clear to the editor, it may not be clear to the reader.

**The policeman's lot**

Often a publisher's editor will crack down about "careless police behavior." Either the police are too stupid, or they are intelligent enough up to a point, then fail to follow up an obvious clue—which would trap your hero, of course, and perhaps that's just what you don't want. These are little brain puzzles that one has to go home and work out on paper, by doodling or by writing down facts from the book once more and seeing how they can be juggled around to fit your story. Maybe the police should be given a less obvious lead. Maybe it is necessary, with a different kind of problem, to visit a local police station and ask about their procedure in certain circumstances.

I was challenged about the rough police behavior in *The Blunderer*, and on the validity of what I had written depended whether *Cosmopolitan* would buy it for condensation. I had spoken earlier to a detective of the homicide squad in Fort Worth, Texas, about this, as I wrote most of the book in Texas. I asked if the police used physical force—blows and truncheons—and I told him exactly how far police brutality went in my book. He endorsed what I had written, saying, with a big smile in which I could see a certain relish, "If we get a guy we have good reason to think is guilty, *we don't hesitate* to work him over." But I went from Greenwich Village, where I was living, to a police station in Lower Manhattan that I was referred to and put the question again to a police official. He also corroborated what I told him I had written, and I was able to tell the *Cosmopolitan* editor that the story had received an official okay.

I had police trouble in *This Sweet Sickness*. Around page one hundred and eighty, the hero has his belongings in suitcases and cartons labeled with his own name, Kelsey, though they have to be picked up from the house where he has been living as "Neumeister." "Neumeister" is practically a recluse in the country house, so the townspeople and tradesmen do not know him by name, but it is still a dangerous thing for him to do, if he does not want the public to know Neumeister and Kelsey are one and the same. The police immediately afterward (but not because of the suitcases) start looking for "Neumeister", whom they have spoken to once, but cannot find again. Kelsey has dropped the Neumeister name and become David Kelsey again in a different town. This was a sticky stretch in the manuscript, which Harper's made me write over, but I fixed it to their satisfaction and mine, though not to my French publisher's, who much to my regret rejected the book with a vague remark that the police were too stupid. Hitchcock bought the story for his hour-long television series. It was called "Annabelle," after the girl Kelsey is in love with. And the book, after slight changes, was published in France by Calmann-Levy.

Of all revisions, the ones concerning police procedure are the hardest work, as they involve technicalities, hard thinking, juggling of plot sometimes, and always sweat.

In *The Story-Teller,* my Doubleday editor made me rewrite the scene in which the hero administers sleeping pills forcibly to the lover of his dead wife. I had Tilbury taking the pills too easily. Tilbury had to put up more of a fight, despite the fact he had not much will to live on that evening.

Typical of a request hard for a beginning writer to take is that he remove a certain character completely from his manuscript—or remove even two characters. These are always minor characters, but they are very likely favorites of the writer, who has lavished much care in depicting them, and quite a few pages on their activities. The trouble with them is that they probably do not advance the plot. Suspense books can scarcely afford characters who do not advance the plot, in spite of the writer's feeling that they vary the pace of the book. This removal of personages means also carefully removing all references to them throughout the manuscript.

For all your cutting, there is usually more to come. Cutting becomes more and more painful, more and more difficult. At last you don't see a single sentence anywhere that can be cut, and then you must say, "Four more whole pages have *got* to come out of this thing," and begin again on page one with perhaps a different colored pencil or crayon in hand to make the recounting easier, and be as ruthless as if you were throwing excess baggage, even fuel, out of an overloaded airplane, as if it were a matter of life or death.

### Serials and condensations

During the time a manuscript is being looked at by a publisher, an agent may be showing a carbon to a magazine which prints books in serial form or condensations of them. Not every book breaks down into convenient episodes for serials, and I don't think it is profitable to try to arrange the story so that it breaks down into four or six serial episodes, unless you have a guarantee that the story will be bought for a serial. *Cosmopolitan* likes writers to do their own condensing to eighty pages, because they believe the author can do it better than anyone else, and I agree. And the handsome sum paid for condensations, $5,000 or $6,000, makes the work seem rather light.

I have condensed *The Blunderer* and *Deep Water* for *Cosmopolitan,* on the first having the handicap of inexperience, on the second that of toothache and interruptions of trips to the dentist, but I think they both came out quite well, and I was especially pleased with *The Blunderer.* On both books I had deadlines, on *The Blunderer* the shorter. I made the initial mistake of trying to copy out portions of *The Blunderer* manuscript with the aim of arriving at the finish on page eighty of my condensation. I sweated and fiddled over this for three days, then realized I was on the wrong track and would have to start over again. The twenty-odd pages I had were jerky, and of no use and were thrown away.

I decided to list eight major points, progressive points in the story, without which the story could not be told. I would take ten pages, and no more, to tell each one. So without looking at the original manuscript, I wrote the book over in this abbreviated form, always with an eye on my list of points and keeping in mind what page of my condensation I was on. The story written in this manner has a freshness that excerpts cannot have. Very often whole sentences, good ones, come out just as they were in the manuscript, because one has remembered them, and the writing goes that much faster. Above all, the sticky and negative process of conscious eliminating and choosing is gone when one does not look at the manuscript.

Line-cutting and word-changing, even on the typewriter, can make a manuscript look finally pretty sloppy. Editors and printers do not mind this, as long as everything is legible. If certain pages are a real mess, I always type them over. I imagine printers, like everyone else, get tired, and I do not like to think of them straining to read something that I could have made more legible with a little more effort. I also remind myself that any manuscript, even a perfectly typed one, looks absolutely awful by the time the copy editor and proofreader have been through it, putting in marginal instructions for the printer. Pages become dog-eared if not grimy, and all in all the manuscript no longer looks like something you want to present with pride to your parents.

If a writer is accessible geographically, he will be asked to look at his own galley proofs and compare them with the now battered manuscript. These galley proofs are narrow and a yard long and are difficult to read outdoors even on a summer day, if there is a breeze. They are difficult to read even on a desk. I think they are easiest read in bed. In these galleys, one is allowed a certain number of changes, a fairly generous number, beyond which the writer will be billed by the publisher. It is foolish to run up a bill, unless one feels very strongly about a certain change, or a number of small changes. It is a mistake beginning writers make, not to do all the changes before the galley stage, and to have second thoughts when the galleys appear in their impressively permanent-looking form.

CHAPTER 10

## ⚡ THE CASE HISTORY OF A NOVEL:
*The Glass Cell*

SINCE I have said quite a bit about suspense fiction, the nature, origin, and development of story ideas, I think it might be useful to discuss here *The Glass Cell*, one of my suspense novels. *The Glass Cell* was not inspired by any specific story idea but evolved simply out of a desire to write such a book—which is perhaps no bad reason for writing a book.

### The germ of an idea

In 1961, I received a letter from a man in prison in the Middle West of the United States. He was thirty-six years old, and in for forgery, breaking and entering, and for breaking parole. It was his third offense, and he had three years to go when he wrote me. These details I learned later, but he had read one of my books called *Deep Water* (I don't think my books should be in prison libraries), and he wrote me a fan letter. He said he was interested in becoming a writer. So began a correspondence between us. In one letter, I asked him to write "My Day" from the time he awakened, or was awakened, until lights-out. He sent back three interesting pages, typewritten, which I still treasure. They told of his joshing, not really chummy relationship with his cell mate, of his work in the shoe factory stapling heels to soles, of what he ate for breakfast, lunch and supper, of the sounds in the cell-block after lights-out at 9:30 P.M. It was the kind of information one cannot get from any book.

A few months later, perhaps because of my prisoner pen pal, I read a book about convicts, a non-fiction book, which told the story of an engineer imprisoned unjustly, a man who was strung up by the thumbs by sadistic guards, and afterward became a morphine addict because of his constant pain. The engineer's wife had remained loyal to him, a rather exceptional thing, but he was so ashamed of his addiction, he could not rejoin her and his family after his release, and went to another city, took a job, and sent money home. Here was part of a story ready-made. But mainly, I felt a desire to write about the atmosphere of a prison. First of all, it would be a challenge to my imagination, a difficult job to do well, even for a man, and a man could at least get into a prison for his research, whereas women are not allowed beyond the corridor bars of a cell-block. I had the advantage of knowing an American criminal lawyer who had many convicts among his clients. He could not get me past the bars, but at least I could wait in the lobby just outside and see the prisoners walking freely in and out of cells whose doors stood open (it was a free period in the afternoon, a time between workshop duty and early supper), and I watched them for perhaps forty minutes. Another source of information was an excellent non-fiction book called *Break Down the Walls,* by John Bartlow Martin.

I began to shape a story. My hero, Philip Carter, would have been in prison ninety days when the book opens—imprisoned through a miscarriage of justice. The stringing up by the thumbs would take place early in the book, perhaps by page eight, and it is precipitated by the difficult and unwritten laws of the prison which Carter, through ignorance, is habitually breaking. His pretty wife, Hazel, visits and writes to him regularly, and every string possible is pulled to get him out, but to no avail. I envisaged a book with the first half set in prison, the latter half out of it, and the second half would show the effects on the character and behavior of a man who had spent six years in a penitentiary among what is known as "bad company." I did not want to have Carter live apart from his wife and small son when he came out. I vaguely saw that Carter might have a rival for his wife's love in the form of a family friend who would also be a lawyer ostensibly trying to help Carter get out of prison.

So much for the germs of this idea, none of them spectacular, all of them intellectual rather than emotional, the first part of the story not even original, but taken from the true story of the wronged engineer.

### Development

The elements in this story were to be: miscarriage of justice; threat of wife's switch of affection to another man; threat of morphine addiction, and consequent possible loss of wife and post-prison job; the deleterious effect of exposure to brutality in prison, and how this can lead to anti-social behavior after release. The process of development, therefore, was to arrange these elements in dramatic form.

Philip Carter, to be in the mess he is in when the story opens, has to be a somewhat easygoing, over-trustful person. He has signed receipts for deliveries of cement, bricks and girders for a building project on which he is an engineer, and he signed them because no one else was handy to sign them, and because a crooked contractor asked him to sign them. The contractor pocketed the difference in price between good materials and inferior ones, the inferior material being what is delivered. When the contractor is accidentally killed on the job, and the shoddiness of the finished building becomes apparent, somebody has to take the blame, and it is Carter, with his name on so many receipts, who does.

Carter's wife, Hazel, is very pretty and also vain, and she is susceptible to the flattery and attention of the attractive young lawyer named David Sullivan—the friend of the family. I would have to invest Sullivan with the qualities Hazel especially admires—discretion, good manners and good taste—to make the pill of betrayal go down (with the reader), because Hazel does have an affair with him. This sets up the emotional machinery for the murder of Sullivan by Carter, not a premeditated murder, but a murder committed in sudden anger. It is a murder, nevertheless, and brings out another of the elements, that prison life can inure a person to brutality, possibly to homicide and to crime in general.

The mystery of who was responsible for the building project fraud had to be clarified eventually. The authorities could find no large sums of money in Carter's bank accounts or in the dead contractor's either, as he has covered his tracks well. But by stating this I had not explained where the money was. Therefore, some person or persons from the building project had to turn up in the second half of the book when Carter is out of prison. I invented Gregory Gawill, a third-rate vice-president of the contracting firm, a man who has visited Carter a couple of times in prison but whom Carter does not trust. Gawill has received a bit of the appropriated money, but he finally discloses that it was the president of the firm who took the lion's share and the crooked contractor who took what was left. Gawill as a character performed three functions for me: messenger of bad tidings to Carter; appropriator of funds and a person who knew the truth about the funds; and an instigator of criminal actions in the latter part of the book. Better to combine these three essentials in one person, if possible, than to spread them over three different characters.

Gawill, from the first of his prison visits, puts the idea in Carter's mind that Hazel is seeing Sullivan too often, and that Sullivan is in love with her. Carter does not know how much of this to believe, but it worries him in prison, for six solid years. And what more natural than that Hazel should tire of sweating it out in a small

Southern town (near the prison) and move back to her
native New York after two years? Sullivan follows her,
and finds a position with a law firm in New York. When
Carter is released and joins his wife in New York, Sullivan is still "just a good friend," but Gawill is around to
prod Carter's imagination, and also to furnish him with
photographs and notes on Hazel's meetings with Sullivan at times when she is supposed to be at her job.
Gawill detests Sullivan, because Sullivan has been
trying, in vain, to pin on him the blame for the
building fraud. Gawill would very much like to whip
Carter up to killing Sullivan. Carter is aware of Gawill's
motive and is amused by it, and has no intention of
obliging him. But Gawill's prodding has its effect.

I intended Carter to commit a serious crime, like
murder. At the same time, perhaps because Carter has
been through so much in prison, I wanted to have him
cleared of his post-prison murder. A double miscarriage
of justice, if you like. I wanted him by some quirk to go
free.

On looking through my notebook, I am amused by
page after page devoted to a floating key, presumably
the key to the whole prison, or at least to some vital
door. The key seems to have circulated freely among
the inmates. It's a rather Kafka-like symbol, I suppose.
It isn't ever used, at least not for a mass escape. Such a
key was not mentioned when I wrote the book. Perhaps
what took its place was a small dog named Keyhole.

Keyhole is a mongrel with some fox terrier in him,
and he is smuggled into the laundry of the prison by a
driver of a prison truck. For months, the dog lives in

the laundry, fed by adoring inmates who bring food from their mess, concealed whenever a guard approaches, known only to the sixty or seventy men who work in the laundry. One day, an inmate steps on the dog in his haste to conceal the dog from a guard, the dog yelps, is discovered, and sent to the pound. A resentment surges in the prison, and news of the dog's existence spreads suddenly among the six thousand prisoners. Two days later, there is a riot—not over the dog exactly, but over the bad conditions in general: the confiscation of the dog only precipitated the outburst. In this riot Carter's only buddy, Max, is senselessly killed. Carter is further embittered by this, and in the remaining four years of his term does not meet anyone else with whom he feels he can form a friendship. This then was the purpose of the dog.

## Plotting

Having gone so far with developing this story, that is, deciding what elements and basic events I wanted in it, the first problem in plotting was where to place them. How much of the book to devote to the prison stretch (we never see Hazel's life outside during this; she only talks and writes to Carter about it); when to have Carter's suspicion of his wife's infidelity confirmed; when to have Carter's murder of Sullivan. Secondly, how to embroil Gawill in all of it and through Gawill somehow arrive at a situation which would miraculously clear Carter of the crime of murdering Sullivan.

The prison should take no more than half the book, I thought. Carter, three-fifths through the book, knows that his wife had and is still having an affair with Sullivan. But Carter holds his temper and his fire. Gawill becomes impatient with Carter's delay in avenging himself on Sullivan and hires a killer, hoping to put the blame on Carter for Sullivan's death. The killer's name is O'Brien, and Carter has met him briefly at Gawill's apartment. It so happens that Carter comes to have a talk with Sullivan—to ask him to end the affair with his wife—the night O'Brien calls on Sullivan to kill him. It is 6 P.M. when Carter is admitted to Sullivan's small apartment house by the release button, and Carter is nearly knocked down by a man who is rushing down the stairs. Sullivan is most upset, tells Carter that he (Carter) saved his life, because a stranger, who rang his doorbell, was about to attack him. Carter is suddenly revolted by Sullivan's cowardice and hypocrisy, picks up the first thing to hand—a Greek marble statue's fragment—and hits Sullivan with it. Carter leaves the apartment and arrives home at more or less the usual time, and the evening goes on as usual until the police telephone at 10 P.M. The police are interested in speaking to Hazel, as they have learned she is a close friend of Sullivan's. In the course of their questions, the police find out that Hazel and Sullivan were more than friends. This turns their suspicions upon Carter, who, they reason, must have been resentful of Sullivan.

What logically or even illogically could happen next? O'Brien, the hired killer, has been thwarted in his assignment. Has O'Brien been paid his fee by Gawill? Does O'Brien think or fear that Carter recognized him ·

as he dashed down Sullivan's stairway? If O'Brien has been paid his fee, he is a lucky man. If he wants to be nasty—and we presume he is nasty or he wouldn't have taken on such a job—he will keep his fee and not tell Gawill anything. If O'Brien hasn't been paid, he can now simply ask for it and presumably get it. I speculated about all this, because the book is seen through Carter's eyes only, and neither Carter nor the reader, therefore, knows what is going on between Gawill and O'Brien. It is Carter who has drawn the conclusion that O'Brien is hired by Gawill.

Let us assume that O'Brien has not yet been paid his fee, and before he can collect, Carter is brought into the picture by the police as a suspect. Also, the same night the police call on Hazel and Carter, they also call on Gawill, because Hazel has given them Gawill's name as "an enemy" of Sullivan's. From now on Gawill and his money transactions will be closely watched, and Gawill knows this.

The police summon Gawill, Carter, and O'Brien— the latter because he is a tough chum of Gawill's, and because the fragment of fingerprint on the Greek marble might be his as well as Carter's—and they are given lie-detector tests. Both Carter and O'Brien come out of this quite well, and the results of the interview are inconclusive for the police.

Carter gets a telephone call from O'Brien, coldly asking him to appear the following Friday evening on a certain street corner in downtown, West Side Manhattan, with five thousand dollars in cash. "Or else, Mr. Carter, and you know what the else is," and O'Brien hangs up. Carter has anticipated this. O'Brien is threatening to tell the police he saw Carter entering Sullivan's house the night of the murder. O'Brien could say, "All right, I was hired to beat Sullivan up, but Carter got there and killed him." Whether O'Brien has been paid by Gawill or not, he is interested in an easy five thousand dollars from Carter.

Carter decides at once not to give O'Brien any money. But if Carter does not appear Friday night, he fears O'Brien will tell the police the story, and that it will sound true. Carter as an ex-convict is suspect per se. If O'Brien tells his story, Carter realizes it is the end of his marriage, his job, his life.

But what if he could kill O'Brien and get away with it? Carter comes to the conclusion that it is his only way out. He has learned some judo-karate in prison. He means to use this.

Carter keeps the appointment Friday evening, persuades O'Brien to walk to a slightly darker street, beats O'Brien severely, and leaves him, making his way via two taxis to Gawill's Long Island apartment.

Gawill is surprised to see Carter but makes him welcome. Gawill has just spent the evening in a local bar. This is at least the fourth visit Carter has made to Gawill's flat. They are far from being bosom friends; in fact they are enemies, but they have a curious liking for each other. Gawill has taunted Carter by saying that he knows he, Carter, killed Sullivan. And Carter has laughed good-naturedly at this. But from the way Gawill has said it, and says it again on this evening, Carter knows that Gawill is lying, and that Gawill believes

O'Brien did it. Carter has behaved "correctly" in destroying the only man besides himself who knew the truth. So on this night when Carter drops in, mainly to give himself an alibi for the evening, the uneasy peace prevails between them as they sit having a drink. The telephone rings at midnight: the police have found O'Brien's body, and what does Gawill know about it? The police are coming over to talk to him.

This is within twenty pages of the end of the book.

Carter talks to Gawill quickly before the police arrive. Gawill has guessed that Carter killed O'Brien, and why: blackmail, and he knows the reason for that. Carter counters with a proposition: He and Gawill must tell the police they spent the evening together in the bar where Gawill was. They must furnish each other with alibis, or Carter will inform the police that Gawill hired O'Brien to kill Sullivan. Gawill sees Carter's point, and when the police arrive, both men stick to the story that they spent the evening together. They stick to it in the days and nights following, when they are grilled separately, and when the police come up with the truth, which they cannot prove. Carter is not at all certain what his wife Hazel will believe, but it is evident when she comes to visit Carter at the jail and he is released, that she has guessed the truth and has forgiven him for what he has done. Hazel and Carter love each other, despite the hardships Carter has put himself and her through, and despite Hazel's infidelity. From the point of view of their marriage lasting, the story ends on a happy note. From the point of view of

Carter's character, it is a depressing story, as it most certainly makes the point that incarceration is damaging to a personality.

I apologize for the dull abbreviation of the story. I made no mention of Carter's son, Timmie, who is twelve years old when Carter is released. Much can be done in such a story by showing the effect of these events on a small child, the child's reactions to his ex-convict father, the attitude of the child's schoolmates toward him. It is horrible and bewildering to a child, but if the child can come round to liking and accepting his father, as Timmie does finally, then something has been won.

### The first draft

The first draft of this book had a somewhat different story line from the one I have summarized, and it got a rejection from Harper & Row. In this first version, as well as in the second version, I committed at least one of the faults that I have talked about earlier in this book. I meant to have the prison part take up half the book, the out-of-prison part the last half. I became so carried away by prison details and events, I soon had nearly two hundred pages of this. It should not have been more than a hundred and twenty pages. A more efficient writer than I would have saved himself the time and effort it took to produce those extra eighty pages.

The beginning, in the prison, went along very well, and the entire prison section remained much the same as it was when *The Glass Cell* was published. In the first version, however, I was on a different tack concerning Carter's murder of Sullivan and its aftermath.

It seems that I was bent (and it was a bad idea) on having Carter ring Sullivan's doorbell, receive no answer but find both the downstairs door and the apartment door unlatched. This can happen with a downstairs door, if someone doesn't close it firmly; with an apartment door, it can't happen, as every New Yorker knows, unless someone has failed to close it (which no murderer inside would do) or unless the button in the lock has been pushed so that the door doesn't lock (which a murderer would scarcely do either). Carter enters the apartment and finds Sullivan dead in his bed, blood coming from a fresh wound. Carter is too frightened of being blamed to call the police, and he is leaving the apartment when he hears a slight noise, like the bump of a shoe, against the closed closet door in the living room. Carter opens the closet and sees a man, a blond man, standing there, a frightened expression on his face, a tumbler half full of whisky in his hand. The man tries to dash out of the closet and escape, but Carter tangles with him, the whisky is spilled—and to end this incident, Carter is not believed when he tells the story to the police.

Where is the blond man? Who is he? Where is the spot on the carpet where the drink spilled, for that matter? (The blond man could have wiped it up, and it would have had time to dry.) Carter is accustomed to taking mild drugs for his still aching thumbs. In prison, he nearly became hooked on morphine. He is suspected of having had an hallucination and of having killed Sullivan. Carter says he ran out of the apartment in a panic. Even his wife doubts him. The blond man is of course a killer hired by Gawill, but Carter had never seen him before the fatal evening. There follows a very sticky time for Carter, as he loses his job and practically loses his wife's allegiance, and the blond man cannot be found. Gawill has the blond man killed, but we don't know this until the blond man's body turns up at a police morgue in Pennsylvania and is identified by Carter—who is delighted with this turn of events, as the blond man's body clears Carter. A more or less happy ending.

I wrote this not only in a first draft, but in a second polished draft, and rather properly the book was rejected by Harper & Row. Carter was a passive, self-pitying, weak and rather stupid hero. We didn't know as much about the blond man as we know in the second version about the hired killer, O'Brien, and though they are not really important as characters, a little about their existence, jobs, attitudes, makes them very much more interesting to the reader.

I now had a rejection on my hands, and either I changed the hero, the story, the whole last half of the book, or it was not going to be accepted by Harper & Row or perhaps by anybody. I thought my story was not bad, but perhaps it could be better. When one thinks this, even faintly, it is best to write it over.

**The snags**

I have discussed my first draft of *The Glass Cell*, which encountered a little more than a snag, and became a disaster. This was caused by my stubborn sticking to a scene I had envisaged, a scene I thought would be good—Carter's finding the murderer of Sullivan by accident in a closet in Sullivan's apartment a few minutes after the murder. I might have realized that unless Carter took some brilliant and energetic action afterward, his part in the story would be a passive one. Passive heroes are bores, unless one makes them deliberately ridiculous and funny, with events and people bumping against them all the time, while they more or less stand still. Carter did not take any more vigorous action than that of looking for the blond man he had seen, and he didn't tramp the streets or the woods doing that, he just kept in touch with the police. This was not enough, and I had to change the story, by making Carter a more active hero.

I had Carter kill Sullivan, and thus I put a terrible but interesting strike against him, considering that I wanted to have the reader "on Carter's side" at the end of the book. Judging from the reviews, I mostly succeeded. Only one reviewer (English) said outright that he was disgusted with Carter's eye-for-an-eye way of thinking, the rest of the reviewers granting, at least tacitly, that prison experiences can harden the sensibilities and conscience in a decent man. I suffered the inevitable snag near the end, when I could not think how to have Carter get away with his killing of the blackmailer

O'Brien and make sure that he would rather "permanently" get away with it, even though the police would always keep Carter on their suspect list.

In such situations, one often has to dovetail the difficulties so that they fit and lock. Invent another crime either of hero or another character, if necessary. In the case of *The Glass Cell*, I used Gawill's less serious crime, the hiring of a killer. Gawill does not want to be blamed for that. Therefore, he and Carter, both guilty, agree to alibi for each other. Such a locked situation appears also in *Strangers on a Train*. By exchanging victims, Guy and Bruno provide each other with genuine alibis: When the murders are committed, each murderer is miles from the scene where his originally intended victim is killed—and can prove it. The essential in this is for the murderers never to see each other again, for it must not be known that they had ever met or known each other. It is a wonder this simple idea is not used more often in real life, and perhaps it is, since it is said that only eleven percent of the murders committed are ever solved.

### The second draft

For practical purposes—selling a book—I shall discuss the second draft of the second version of *The Glass Cell*, which was eventually published.

I had a great deal of cutting to do in the first half, which took place in the prison, and much of this was painful, as I thought this part interesting. (As it was, I did not cut it enough to suit my editor, and more had to be cut later, down to 105 pages.) Most of my cuts were solid paragraphs of description, not involving people.

There was a dull stretch in the book once Carter was out of prison, getting used to civilian life or trying to, and looking for a job. The only active factor in this section was his looking for a job. I took too much time describing his trip from the prison by bus to the town where he caught the plane to New York, his arrival in New York and his welcome by Hazel and Timmie at the airport, the dinner that evening in the pleasant apartment Hazel has created and which Carter has never seen before.

The only important thing in this section really is that Sullivan is present at the airport to welcome Carter, too, and declines an invitation from Hazel to dine with them that evening. Carter feels a surge of jealousy, of suspicion, not diminished by his finding a couple of Sullivan's law books in the bedroom later that evening. This is of emotional importance, and after all, a novel is an emotional thing. All this was cut from twelve pages to five. But that was not the end of the dull stretch. I had to cut more in the pages that followed in which Carter answers ads for engineers' positions. Nothing really *happens* until Gawill turns up "accidentally" on the street in front of Carter's house and manages to fill Carter's head again with stories about his wife's carrying on with Sullivan. Only this action, in all this stretch of predictable events, really advances the plot.

In this second version, Carter was a much stronger character than he had been in the first, and I tackled head on the subtle but vital matter of his relationship with Hazel. Carter adores her, despite the fact he knows she is having an affair. Hazel loves Carter, too, and feels not so much passion for Sullivan as—real love. Sullivan and she have been close for six years, all the time Carter was in prison. Sullivan was Hazel's friend and counselor as well as her lover, and his presence buoyed her up over the long, depressing years. Sullivan and the boy Timmie like each other very much. The affair between Hazel and Sullivan is not a fly-by-night thing. At the same time, Hazel can hardly make speeches to Carter about how much she loves Sullivan, since she wants to maintain her marriage with Carter. Life has forced on her or given her the ability to love two people.

This is difficult to put into words; Hazel doesn't try, but it must all be implied. Carter and Hazel have two or three crucial conversations around and on this problem, which do not solve it, unfortunately, for Hazel does not really promise to "give up" Sullivan. These conversations have to be written properly in the first draft, I think, as they are difficult to tinker with afterward. On reading over such conversations, you may find them phony, or crude, or vague, or possibly so delicate that the reader can't really tell what you are writing about. In such cases, it is better to scrap the pages and write them afresh.

I did not make any story changes in my second draft of *The Glass Cell*, but retyped much of the last half, condensing conversation and actions—such as Carter organizing a week's holiday in New England for himself and Hazel and Timmie, just after the Sullivan murder, in order to get them both out of the New York atmosphere of police questions and friends' suspicions. Nothing happens on this week's vacation except that Hazel maintains her coolness, her waiting attitude, in regard to Carter, whose guilt she suspects. This is not worth more than a page, and that is how long it is.

And then once again I must read through the whole book with its retyped pages, its clarified passages, its cuttings, and see how it sounds. New faults may strike the eye. And the process of rewriting and clarifying and cutting and emphasizing must start all over again, with new notes. There is one consolation: there is less to do each time.

### Revisions

The revisions on *The Glass Cell* were not major, but after all, I had written the book three or four times by then, if I count the first version which was rejected.

I was asked by my editor to check again the amount of morphine used in an average hospital dose to stop pain, the amount taken by addicts, and so forth. This had to be accurate, so even though I thought I had been accurate, I went back to the library's medical reference books. To be on the safe side, I finally decreased the number of grains taken by Carter daily in prison. I was also asked to lower Carter's salary from the Southern contracting firm, to lower his salary in New York, and to reduce his income from the legacy left him by an aunt. I don't know why I made these amounts too high, as I usually make them too low, and I cite them here only as an example of what one may be asked to do by an editor. It is not wise to argue, since the editor probably knows better than you and has had the advantage of discussing the matters with several other people in the publishing house. It is surprising how many beginning writers blow their stacks over trivial requests like these or over being asked to remove a character from a book. Sometimes they quit agents in a huff or withdraw their manuscripts from publishers. Very often they have to come crawling back. A writer's life is absolutely full of places to show pride, much more difficult and important places than these.

This was not the first book over which I had come a cropper. Another was *The Two Faces of January*, which was quite a mess in its first version (not the one I described earlier), and received the comment from Harper & Row along with its rejection, "A book can stand one or even two neurotics, but not three who are the main characters." I let time go by and wrote another book, which was accepted, and then returned to *January* and rewrote it, but without referring to the first manuscript, because I completely changed the plot, the age and character of the wife and the character of the young hero—everything except the layout of the Palace of Knossos; three-quarters of a page was all I used of the first manuscript. The charm of that musty old hotel in Athens and the fascination of the young man on meeting a stranger who resembled his father (and a stranger who was a crook), these still held me fascinated, and inspired me to write another two hundred and fifty or three hundred pages in order to use these characters. This second and present version of *The Two Faces of January* was also rejected out of hand by Harper & Row, and this time I thought they were wrong, though I shelved the book, mentally at least, and did not know what to do except write another book. These little setbacks, amounting sometimes to thousands of dollars' worth of time wasted, writers must learn to take like Spartans. A brief curse, perhaps, then tighten the belt a notch and on to something new—of course with enthusiasm, courage and optimism, because without these three elements, you cannot produce anything good.

I heard the news about the second version of *January* while in Positano in June of 1962. I remember I was surprised and baffled, but somehow not downcast. After all, it was my seventh or eighth book, I had had rejections before, and rejections do become easier to bear as time goes on. More important, I for once thought I was right about liking the book; I did not feel I had done a shoddy piece of work, or written a boring book. But I did nothing about the book, went back home, and began to think about my prison book. A few months later, I was in London briefly, and gave my publishers, Heinemann, a ring. While having a drink with a Heinemann editor in a pub, I mentioned the *January* rejection. "Let us see it," said the Heinemann editor. I did, and Heinemann published it as it stood.*

Harper & Row rejected *The Glass Cell* in its second and final version in early 1964. This left me with two

---

* Later *The Two Faces of January* was selected by the Crime Writers Association of England as the best foreign crime novel of 1964, and received a prize at their Annual Award Dinner. Such is the strange fate of a twice-rejected book.

books rejected by Harper & Row, both of which I thought were good and in publishable form. So reluctantly—no writer likes to switch publishers, and writers should do as little of this as possible—I tried Doubleday, submitting a page-proof dummy of *The Two Faces of January* from the Heinemann Press, and it was accepted. Usually, it is America who publishes my books first, then England, so this was an exceptional case. I then had to cut forty pages from it and rewrite page twelve and paste it into the dummy. It gives one a strange feeling to cut and alter a manuscript that already looks like a printed book, but it is much easier to handle, and easier to count the lines cut. I must have gone through the dummy thirty times before arriving at the proper count—one thousand three hundred and twenty lines cut, which amounted to forty pages.

In April of 1964, I showed the Harper-rejected manuscript of *The Glass Cell* to my Doubleday editor, who was in London working at the Doubleday office there. It was accepted, too, and again I had to cut forty pages, and from the manuscript. The manuscript looked quite blackened with crayon lines, plus red ones from a second cutting attack. Some pages had only three lines of printable prose on them, the rest resembling the British Union Jack, but at least what was left was legible.

**The book**

The Sunday *New York Times* review began stickily, "I don't know quite what to make of Miss Highsmith's . . ." and ended with, "Better try it yourself and see what you think." Not a complimentary phrase in it that could be used in an advertisement.

*The New York Herald-Tribune* did not review it at all, and neither did *The New Yorker*. I received from out of town good or very good reviews from the *Times-Picayune* of New Orleans, and the *Pittsburgh Press* which said ". . . extraordinary by anybody's standards." The Virginia Kirkus Bulletin, well known in the book trade, called it my "best book since *Strangers on a Train*." Although there has been no movie or reprint interest in the States, the sales are more than seven thousand and climbing nicely; I would think this is due to my general reputation rather than to the reviews of this book.

In England, the reviews were much better and appeared in all the important newspapers and weekly reviews. My publishers at the outset had tripled the number of copies printed of *The Two Faces of January*, the book which preceded this, which meant ten thousand copies. Pan Books, which reprinted my books at that time in England, contracted for *The Glass Cell*, and it appeared in softcover about a year after the original hardcover edition.

CHAPTER 11

## ⚡ THE BOOK

AFTER all the work we have been doing, at least theo-
retically, in shaping and writing a book, we might treat
ourselves to imagining a finished product, a book that
is finally between covers, and see what will happen to
it.

First, let's imagine the fate of the average suspense
novel, a first novel.

*The New York Times* Sunday *Book Review* may give
it an inch and a half or two inches of review under
Mystery and Suspense, and after a non-committal sketch
of the plot, which fills nine-tenths of the review, the last
sentence may be: "Weak finish mars an otherwise promising first book." The publishers have been waiting for
a nice quote to put in their ad, and the best they possibly can do with this is "promising first book," which
is not very eye-catching and barely ethical to use.

In a few weeks, reviews from all over the country will

straggle in, sent you by your publishers, from the *San Francisco Chronicle,* the *New Orleans Times-Picayune,* the *Miami News,* the *Wichita Eagle,* the *Pittsburgh Press,* and other newspapers you may never have heard of, and you are afraid most people have never heard of them and will never read them, either. These reviews may be as long as five inches, and some are quite wonderful, but how many people are going to see them? Well, at least a *few* people see them.

If you live in New York, you are longing for *The New Yorker* to give your book even two inches of comment in their Mystery and Crime column which appears once a month. If they do, and it is a favorable review, this is a piece of luck, as applause from them looks very good in an ad.

### Advertising and sales

After a month, you may make an anxious call to your publishers to ask how sales are going and learn that hardly four hundred of the five thousand copies printed have been sold. You picture it on bookshelves everywhere, not being bought, then you ring the publishers again, and demand an ad, since it seems to you the complete absence of advertising, apart from a tiny billing in the *Times* along with fifteen other authors of your publishing house, is the logical explanation for the lack of sales. Perhaps by now another paper has reviewed you and more favorably than the *Times,* and you would like to see an ad with a phrase from that review: "Suspense well held," for instance. The publishers will explain matter-of-factly that they have an advertising budget, that yours is used up for the moment, but another ad will be forthcoming in about a month. This is far from satisfactory to a new author. Experienced writers learn not to pester publishers about ads. It is only annoying to publishers, makes you look amateurish, and anyway it is quite true that they have a budget.

I know one writer who became rather comically paranoid about the lack of ads for his first book (after a glowing review in a big New York Sunday paper) and fired off at least thirty letters, each of some length, to different publishers in New York, denouncing the treachery of his publishers in not pushing his book, and enclosing a photostatic copy in each letter of his glowing review. I think his publishers were glad to let him go, and the other publishers were afraid to take him on. The businesslike way to secure advertising is to have the matter out first with your publisher, before the book is published. Tell them what you would like—and they will tell you what they can afford. More advertising can be demanded, if the book is a strong one. But some of the best authorities (Alfred A. Knopf, for example, after fifty-two years of publishing) admit that they don't know whether advertising or word of mouth is more important in selling a book.

You have probably been paid an advance against royalties of $1500 on signing the contract, of which you retain $1350, if you have an agent. (The agent's commission is usually ten per cent.) This sum probably could not keep you sheltered and fed during the time it took you to write the book, so as this dawns on you, plus the fact that months go by after the book is published and *nothing* happens, you feel more and more down in the mouth. Paperback people haven't nibbled. Hollywood is silent. No luck selling the book in England, much less in France. After nearly a year, you may receive a royalty check for $119.47. And that is that. That is the average book, even one that got fairly good reviews and not a single bad review.

The fact is, a first book is usually a financial loss for the writer, and quite often for the publisher, too. A publisher hopes, and usually believes, that a writer will go on writing, that he will improve, that his reputation will grow. It is the growth potentiality that the publisher considers when he meets you; he is not looking merely at your manuscript. If he doesn't meet you, he will very likely be interested in your age, and what kind of life you are leading now—as this has to do with how much and how soon you can logically produce.

Fifteen years ago, I estimated that I had to have $3,000 laid by before embarking on a book, because it cost me this to live for the eight or ten months it might take to write the book. By now the cost of living has more than doubled, while the basic advance, $1500, remains the same. A first book is a luxury, more of a luxury than a trip to Europe.

### Agents

I am sometimes asked if it is wise to have an agent or not. The going story is, and I believe it, that every book manuscript sent to a publishing house, or every legible short story that is sent to a magazine, will get a fair reading. In that case, one shouldn't need an agent **for a**

first book. The problems come later, and immediately if
the book is accepted. I think it would take a scrupu-
lously ethical publishing house to tell a new author
what clauses in the contract are customarily struck out.
The author is assumed able to read, but it can also be
assumed that he will be shy about asserting himself in
regard to a first contract. The clauses that are usually
struck out of standard contracts have to do with the
publisher's taking a percentage of movie money, overseas sales, television adaptation money and other income from the book. If one has a "model contract"
from a writer friend to go by, a contract in which these
clauses have been struck out, then one might do all
right after comparing royalty scales with those of the
model contract. Publishers will probably not argue if
you ask to have these clauses out, but they will probably
not call your attention to them, either. I am certainly in
favor of having an agent after the book is published,
because an agent can find overseas markets much better
than a writer—who is apt to be a blank on publishers in
Sweden and Denmark, for instance—and an agent will
take care of all the tedious business of covering letters
for the book, postage, and arguing over the size of advances.

Publishers will also contact the agent about publicity,
arrangements for radio and television appearances, because they know the agent has had experience in these
things. Or the agent will get in touch with broadcasting
studios and newspaper people on a writer's behalf.
Agents also know about short story markets, changes in
editorships of magazines and publishing houses, and

how they will affect their clients, because this is part of their business. When a writer's books start selling as far afield as Japan, he is very glad to have an agent handling all these details that would otherwise take up his mornings and a good deal of energy in letter writing, book wrapping and trips to the post office.

But it is a mistake to leave everything to the agent—especially the selling of oneself—as many writers are inclined to do. They think they have at last got someone who will push them, and they can sit back and relax. Many writers are introverted and shy and detest pushing themselves. But such writers can at least sit home and *think* about ways to push themselves, because, after all, an agent has at least seventy-five people on his list besides you. A writer may be on good terms with a bookshop owner, for instance, who will give him a window display or a small autographing party when his book comes out. If a writer is living in New York, but was born somewhere else in America, his home-town newspaper might be delighted to run a photograph of him plus a sizable review of his book (if he has not lampooned everybody in town) and a short biography about him. "Local boy makes good." All these little things are important.

A few years ago, I resolved virtuously to do something, one little thing every month, for my "public relations." I did not know exactly what to do every month to push myself, and I often hated thinking about it, but I made myself think of some small thing and carry it out. Sometimes it was no more than a letter to my English agent asking about the current market for suspense stories in slick magazines; or a letter or a telephone call to my American agent asking what was the matter with Italy lately, or what could be done about Italy, because they hadn't bought a book since so-and-so; or possibly I thought of a market for a short story to suggest to my agent. A letter to an overseas agent will gain you some information, and also let the overseas agent know you are still alive, which is easy for remote agents to forget between books.

One day, I could think of no way to push, no way at all. *The Talented Mr. Ripley,* which had recently appeared in the United States, had been rejected by my French publishers, and consequently my French translator, Jean Rosenthal of Paris, had never seen the book. I hardly knew M. Rosenthal at that time, but I liked him, and sent him this book in English as a little present by way of my "public relations" for that month. After all, the business of pushing oneself is not always as vulgar as it sounds. It is a way of letting the world or anyone know that you exist; it is a gesture of communication. So I sent the book off to Paris. Weeks later, I learned that M. Rosenthal had liked it, and had shown it again to Calmann-Levy, my French publishers, who had had second thoughts about it, and had decided to publish it. Therefore Ripley saw the light of French print as *M. Ripley.* Without this small gesture of friendliness on my part, the book would not have been printed in France, would not have won a Grand Prix, and would not have been made into a film. A few minutes' effort had brought me thousands of dollars and quite some renown.

### Earnings and taxes

It is curious that with all the work that goes into a book, and the personal attention a writer gives it, the Department of Internal Revenue has decreed that writers' royalties are unearned income (Tax Guide for U.S. Citizens Abroad, paragraph on *Royalties*), and that they must be taxed at the same rate as stock dividends that people have no hand in at all, or income from inherited trusts or leased houses. Rather, the Internal Revenue Department has decided there are two kinds of books, and favors the "businessman" kind of writer rather than the "artistic" kind. For instance, if a writer walks into a publishing house and talks up a book he *intends* to write, sells the idea outright, and goes home and writes it, the money he has received is earned. If he writes the book first, then sells it, as most writers do, the royalties therefrom are unearned, and are regarded as "rent" or "the leasing of your property"—in this case, your intellectual product. While they are on this tack, I am sure the Authors Guild and hundreds of writers all over America would like them to pursue it a bit further and get after the lending libraries who buy a few copies of our intellectual product and proceed to rent it ad infinitum, pocketing all returns and never giving a cent to the authors. Such genteel piracy, too—most of these lending libraries all over the country being run by nice old ladies, bibliophiles themselves.

But to look at it philosophically, writing a book is a gamble, it just happens to be a rather serious one for most writers, involving not only themselves but their families, for better or worse. And perhaps with the unearned income category, writing moves nearer to being considered a business, and business is apt to be protected by the Department of Internal Revenue, as far as bankruptcy and the spreading of losses and rein-vestment of profits are concerned. At present, if a writer takes a loss in one year—that is, doesn't earn ex-penses because of a rejection or the fact that he has not finished his book—he is allowed no relief on the tax of the next year, which might be a better year, whereas a business owner would be. As a writer-contributor to the Authors Guild *Bulletin* recently pointed out, a man can take an author's works when they are in public domain, re-publish them and sell them, and if he goes bankrupt he is protected, because he in business, though the au-thor may well have gone bankrupt and died rather un-comfortably during the same period.

If a writer has a very good year, there is barely one chance in four that his production pattern will fit the precise government requirements permitting this in-come to be spread. If a writer has a bonanza year, it is worth his hiring an accountant—and one who knows writers' problems—to investigate the tax situation, for nowhere in the forms will he find all his rights spelled out.

The Authors Guild of America is fighting a long battle about these matters and has succeeded in getting a law through that if a writer's income in one year is more than 100% of the total of the three preceding years' income, the income can be spread.

This is a big step in the right direction, but does not help the great number of writers whose up periods are not so spectacular, and whose down periods are on the borderline of poverty. In 1959, for no reason except chance, my income was between nine and ten times my income for 1958, a year when I had no tax because my income was so low. The law about spreading was not in effect then. Unless tax laws are adjusted still further, it is next to impossible for a writer to lay much by for his declining years.

However, to imagine the fate of a luckier book than the first, it might be this: favorable reviews in both the *Times* and the *New York Times Book Review,* with some phrases like "Miss —— has a flair for the macabre" or "Mr. ——'s first venture into suspense set me shivering," from which the publishers can extract shorter phrases for their ad which will appear the following day, the day the book is on sale. *The New Yorker* may have found room, and their comment may end with the valuable cachet "highly recommended." Hollywood takes notice. So do the reprint houses. A reprint sale can come within a week of publication, or it may take six months or a year.

### Reprints

The reprint sale may be $4,000, of which you get fifty percent and your publisher fifty percent, paid in possibly three installments over a period of a year and a half. An independent Hollywood producer may ask for an option of one year, for which he will pay $1,000 against a final price of $10,000. Your publisher, or your agent, if you have one, will try to raise this to $17,500 by saying he already has an offer of $10,000, and you and he are not willing to sell for $10,000. It is doubtful if a first book can be raised any higher. It is impossible to point out coolly that your last book sold for $7,500, because there wasn't any. So you agree to the $10,000 and receive the option money. Half the time, this option never materializes into a movie. The producer may not find enough backers, the trend in Hollywood may change and be anti-suspense after a year has gone by. Still, you have the $1,000, and after a year the property is free for another possible buyer.

Meanwhile, a London publishing house has bought your book. Your advance from England will be about $400, as their printings are smaller. The good luck may stop here. You have taken in, roughly, $4,665 after agent's commission, if we assume the first royalty check was about $300, and perhaps it didn't cost you $4,665 to live while writing the book, if you write quickly—although a year and a half or two years may have passed since the day you got the germ of the idea for it. I am considering writing time here as actual writing time, not thinking time. But what is more important than the money, you have made a bigger splash than the vast majority of first suspense novels make.

And long before the year's option is up, you should be working on another book. In fact, some writers say the best way to cushion the blows of reviews is to be completely engrossed in writing another book when they appear. The only way to get ahead, the only reliable way, in suspense writing, is to create a backlog of published books. Of course, flukes can happen, such as a movie sale of $20,000, a magazine condensation or a serial before publication which brings in $6,000, but mostly these things don't happen.

My income is usually one-third from the United States and two-thirds from other countries combined—England, France, Sweden, Denmark, Norway, Germany, Holland. Except for England and France, these countries offer only about $200 each as advance against royalties, but the saving grace is that there are so many of them. I even forgot Brazil and Spain—two different languages again. I often think of all the translators and printers I give work to, and I am pleased to be contributing to their income.

With five books behind you, your life is very different from that of a writer with only one book behind him. It is next to impossible to live on one book—that is, give up one's job—immediately after it is published, though I tried it, as my commercial work had become very irksome to me, and I had a lot of new pride in becoming "a writer," and I had also the advantage of a movie sale of my first book (*Strangers on a Train*) to Alfred Hitchcock, though for a sum so small no one believes it when I quote it, so I won't here. My life was all right for about a year and a half; I went to Europe in a modest way, and began a second book on a freighter on the way back. But the going was very rough for three years after that; I did not have the comforts I had grown used to while doing hack work, though I was producing books at the rate of not quite one a year and occasionally selling a short story. 1953 was particularly grim, but since I was alone, I stuck it out. I wanted to be able to say to myself that I had done no hack work since my first book was published. I had rather work in a department store, as I did once, than try to write fact stories or hack fiction. It is not that I think it corrupting to one's own writing, but I find it dishonest and disgusting.

With five books published, you begin to feel much more important, secure, and in communication with the world at last. Contracts from foreign countries pop into your mailbox, each bringing a welcome $200, and twice a year when the royalties are due, there are more trickles—sometimes only $37.50, or even $4.19—but then, there are several of them. Italy may ask to buy a book which they will abbreviate themselves (best not to ask how) to appear in a Sunday newspaper supplement. The payment for this may be as low as $80.

Lots of suspense writers sell their books directly to paperback houses, thereby doubling or tripling their income. This is a matter of personal preference. I like to see my books in hardcover first. I think more attention is paid in Europe to a hardcover book than to a paperback, and that therefore there is more likelihood of a sale in Europe. But it is obviously tougher economically (at least at first) to write for hardcover, as one has to split the money with the publisher in case of a reprint sale. The Authors Guild is trying to secure better terms for the writer in this, too—a sixty-forty split, for instance, in favor of the writer. This is important to the average writer who writes average books, because how this particular reprint sum (always bigger than the hardcover advance) is split can mean the difference between his having to take a job or not, between his living modestly but decently, or living badly and perilously. It is a depressing thought that "the average writer" cannot live an average life, support a wife and one or two children decently, if his books have only average reception and sales. Yet the world is full of average plumbers, barbers, salesmen who do adequately on their incomes, and without anxiety. The latest figure I can find on "writers in America who support themselves entirely by writing fiction" is two hundred and fifty, which is still very low. A writer with a wife and family must either possess a wonderful knack for obtaining odd writing jobs, for doing part-time work of any kind, or he must simply hold down a job and write in the evenings and on weekends.

I think if an unmarried writer is having a low period financially, it is more costly to try to share expenses with someone than to live alone. If one lives with someone, one's standard of living is apt to rise, while one's working time is cut. This more than offsets the sharing of expenses, which can be a variable factor, while the other two are usually invariable. It is not fair to ask or logical to expect that an ordinary person will undergo the privations that writers and painters, artists of any kind, and many scientists and inventors will accept as a matter of course, even lightheartedly. People who take some degree of comfort and security for granted have a different attitude toward life and fate from that of the free-lance artist, and their goals are completely different. Security is a goal for many people, and while it may be the goal of a writer, it is pretty far down on his list of goals. The majority of people are interested in higher pay, longer vacations, and early retirement. A writer may be very much interested in higher pay, but he is *anti* the other two things, and in fact early retirement, necessitated by his failing powers, would be only a tragedy to him.

Writers and painters like their work for its own sake, while a great many people work only because they have to; therefore stopping it while they "still have some time to enjoy life" becomes a desideratum. People with this goal start earlier than they think, which is why they find the sometimes comfortless life of an artist intolerable if they are forced to share it. It is not true that artists are not disciplined. They are sometimes emotionally undisciplined, because some never grow up emotionally, but when it comes to their work and working habits, the only calling that can touch theirs in dedication is the priesthood. Their whole turn of mind is religious in the sense of the root of the word, that they are bound to something, in this case to the writer's calling.

CHAPTER 12

## ﹏✄ Some Notes on Suspense
in General

I MENTIONED earlier the scope that exists within the suspense genre, but merely the need (which I feel) to point this out is absurd and unfortunate. I hope there will be some readers of this book who do not intend to be suspense writers, but simply writers, because I think much of what I have said applies to writing in general, the writing of fiction, at least. The suspense label which America, American booksellers, and American reviewers are so fond of is only a handicap to the imagination of young writers, like any category, like any arbitrary law. It is confining where there should be no confinement. Young writers should be doing something new, not for newness' sake, but because their imaginations are fresh and free. Murderers, psychopaths, prowlers-in-the-night are old hat, unless one writes about them in a new way.

### The "suspense" label

I would like to write a novel—which will inevitably be labeled a suspense novel in America—which has no murderer, no crime, no violent action. I very nearly did it in *The Story-Teller*. And also in *Those Who Walk Away*, which was concerned with the people *around* a presumed murderer, and their attitudes, rather than with the murderer himself. It was about a man who believes he is doomed to die at the hands of one or two other people, who suffers a consequent anxiety, but does not meet this fate at all. I am interested in what kind of judgments the people involved will pass on one another.

To illustrate what I mean about categories, I must cite once more my first book, *Strangers on a Train*, which was just "a novel" to me when I wrote it, and yet when it sold, was labeled "suspense novel." Thenceforth, I found myself in this category, which means also to find oneself fated to no more than three-inch-long reviews in the newspapers, squeezed in among good and bad books which get the same brief treatment—and by bad books, I mean the books of careless hacks. In college, when I was writing short stories, half might have been what is now called suspense and half not, but no one used the term on the college magazine, and when one of these college-written stories, "The Heroine," sold to *Harper's Bazaar* and later went into an O. Henry Prize Story collection, no one said that I had written a suspense story, though "The Heroine" certainly is one by book trade standards. Of my short stories, more than half of which do not sell, only half can be called suspense stories by any stretch of the term. Those that sell are not necessarily "suspense" stories. The suspense label does no one any good.

In France and England, I am not particularly categorized as a suspense novelist, just as a novelist, and I fare much better as to prestige, quality of reviewing and —proportionally speaking—in sales than in America. In England, my books are reviewed by people of some repute, either as writers or critics or both, and often one of my books gets a thousand-word review in a column to itself. The word "thriller" or "suspense" is generally not used. In France, a full-page critique in a literary newspaper, or a half-page in a newspaper is not unusual, and four of my books have been or will be reprinted in the distinguished Hachette series, Livres de Poche, which include the world's classics. I cannot account for the difference in reception of my books in America and in Europe except perhaps by pointing out the most obvious difference: the glut of the market in America with mediocre suspense and mystery novels in hardcover and paperback, but especially in paperback. My advice to young and beginning writers, if they wish to stay free agents, is to keep as clear of the suspense label as possible.

One of my editors once remarked to me that suspense and mystery books have a floor and a ceiling of sales, meaning that a certain number of any such books will be bought, no matter how bad they are. One thinks of people in a hurry at a railroad station, sweeping up an armful of anything from the newsstand for the journey. This is the floor. The ceiling is presumably determined by the fact that many book buyers would never dream of buying a mystery or suspense book, in hardcover or paperback. Mystery and suspense books have a circumscribed readership. The floor is nice, of course, but the ceiling is not nice, and one can't have this particular floor without this particular ceiling. There are some exceptions to the sales pattern, *The Spy Who Came in from the Cold* by John le Carré, for instance.

But there is no doubt that in America the suspense and mystery book has a cheapness hanging about it, a reputation for superficiality, a stigma of inferiority to the straight novel, which is just as automatically assumed to be more serious, important, and worthwhile because it is a straight novel and because the author is assumed to have a serious intent in writing it. Is one to blame the writers for this, or the publishers, or both? Since books begin with writers, writers should begin to try to change this. It is for this reason really—mediocrity —that most suspense books and therefore their writers can never be real best sellers, never break through.

### Marks of quality

The suspense writer can improve his lot and the reputation of the suspense novel by putting into his books the qualities that have always made books good—insight, character, an opening of new horizons for the imagination of the reader. I do not speak, in this paragraph, about mystery books, because they are out of my line, and it is a characteristic of them that the identity of the murderer is withheld, or at any rate his character as murderer is not deeply explored, if at all. If a suspense writer is going to write about murderers and victims, about people in the vortex of this awful whirl of events, he should do more than describe brutality and gore and the gooseflesh in the night. He should throw some light on his characters' minds; he should be interested in justice or the absence of it in the world we live in; he should be interested in the morality, good and bad, that exists today; he should be interested in human cowardice or courage, and not merely as forces to push his plot this way and that. In a word, his people should be real. This seriousness may sound at variance with the element of playing that I mentioned in regard to plot, but it is not, since I am talking of another matter. The spirit of playing is necessary in plotting to permit freedom of the imagination. It is also necessary in inventing characters. But once one *has* the characters in mind, and the plot, the characters should be given most serious consideration, and one should pay attention to what they are doing and why, and if one does not explain it —and it may be artistically bad to explain too much— then a writer should know why his characters behave as they do and should be able to answer this question to himself. It is by this that insight is born, by this that the book acquires value. Insight is not something found in psychology books; it is in every creative person. And— see Dostoyevsky—writers are decades ahead of the textbooks, anyway.

It often happens that a writer has a theme or a pattern in his books, and he should be aware of this, though again not in a hampering way. He should be aware of it so as to exploit it well, and so as not to repeat it without realizing it. Some writers' themes may be a quest for something—a father one never knew, the pot of gold which does not exist at the foot of the rainbow. Others may have a recurrent girl-in-distress motif, which starts them off plotting, and without which they are not exactly comfortable writing. Another is a doomed love or a doomed marriage. Mine is the relationship between two men, usually quite different in make-up, sometimes obviously the good and the evil, sometimes merely ill-matched friends. I might have realized this theme in myself at least by the middle of *Strangers on a Train*, but it was a friend, a newspaperman, who pointed it out to me when I was twenty-six and just beginning *Strangers*, a man who had seen the manuscript of my first effort at twenty-two that I have already mentioned, the book that was never finished. This was about a rich, spoiled boy, and a poor boy who wanted to be a painter. They were fifteen years old in the book. As if that weren't enough, there were two minor characters, a tough, athletic boy who seldom attended school (and then only to shock the school with things like the bloated corpse of a drowned dog he had found on the banks of the East River) and a puny, clever boy who giggled a great deal and adored him and was always in his company. The two-men theme turned up also in *The Blunderer*, *The Talented Mr. Ripley*, in *A Game for the Living*, and *The Two Faces of January*, and raises its head a little in *The Glass Cell* in the curious comrades-in-social-defiance attitude between Carter and Gawill. So in six books out of ten it has turned up, certainly in my "best" books in public opinion. Natural themes cannot be sought or strained for; they appear. Unless one is in danger of repeating oneself, they should be used to the fullest, because a writer will write better making use of what is, for some strange reason, innate.

For example, the one really dull book I have written was my fifth, *A Game for the Living*, in which the murderer (of the girl found dead in Chapter One) is but dimly introduced early in the story. He is not to be suspected. Another man, whom we know much better, confesses, though his confession is not entirely believed. The real murderer is off-scene mostly, so *A Game for the Living* became a "mystery who-dunnit" in a way— definitely not my forte. I had tried to do something different from what I had been doing, but this caused me to leave out certain elements that are vital for me: surprise, speed of action, the stretching of the reader's credulity, and above all that intimacy with the murderer himself. I am not an inventor of puzzles, nor do I like secrets. The result, after rewriting the book four times in a grueling year of work, was mediocrity. I always say to foreign publishers, and to publishers who contemplate a reprint, "This is my worst book, so please think twice before you buy it." However, I believe that any story can be told properly, using some of the writer's stronger points, but the writer must first be aware of what his stronger points are. I disobeyed my natural laws in this boring book, and it was unforgivable of me.

I have said little about other people's suspense books, mainly because I seldom read them, and so I am unqualified to say that certain suspense books are good, very good, or why. I like best Graham Greene's entertainments, mainly because they are intelligent, and their prose is very skillful. He is also a moralist, even in his entertainments, and I am interested in morality, providing it isn't preached. There is no doubt that a study of the whole field of "the best" in suspense writing, whatever that is, can be of benefit professionally to a suspense writer, but I would just as soon not pursue this study. After all, I do not take myself seriously as a suspense writer as to category, and I am not interested in seeing how another writer handled a difficult theme successfully, because I cannot keep his or her example in my mind when I am faced with my typewriter and my own problem. I read Graham Greene's novels for pleasure, but I do not ever think of imitating him or even of being guided by him— except that I would like to have his talent for *le mot juste,* a gift that can be admired in Flaubert, too. And given this laziness about studying my own field, it is easy to rationalize and excuse it by telling myself I believe I run a danger of copying if I read other people's suspense books. I don't really believe this. There is no enthusiasm in copying, and without enthusiasm, one can't write a decent book.

### The sense of joy

I end this with a terrible feeling I have left something out, something vital. I have. It is individuality, it is the joy of writing, which cannot really be described, cannot be captured in words and handed to someone else to share or to make use of. It is the strange power that work has to transform a room, any room, into something very special for a writer who has worked there, sweated and cursed and maybe known a few minutes of triumph and satisfaction there. I have many such rooms in my memory—a tiny one in Ambach, near Munich, with a ceiling so low I could not stand up at one end of it, formerly a maid's room, in an inn; a freezing, leaky room in an English coastal town, a room whose cracks I used to plug up desperately as if I were in a sinking ship; a room in Florence with a wood stove that was determined not to burn anything; a room in Rome whose interior, when I recall it, evokes a memory of hard work and bedlam curiously combined. It is the lonely nature of writing that these strong memories and emotions cannot be shared with anyone.

On the pleasant side, there is the sense of being completely and happily engrossed in a book while writing it, whether the writing takes six weeks, six months or much longer. One must protect a book while writing it —it is a bad mistake, for instance, to show part of it to someone who you are pretty sure is going to be a cruel critic, and therefore possibly damage your confidence in yourself—but in its way the writing of the book will protect you from all kinds of emotional blows, of a destructive kind, which otherwise might wound and distract.

The precariousness and detachedness of a writer's existence has its reverse side when our fortunes rise a little: we can fly over to Majorca for a couple of weeks in the sun, off-season, when our friends are stuck in the city. Or we can join a friend who is sailing in a ramshackle boat from Acapulco to Tahiti and not worry about how long the voyage will take—and possibly we

will get a book out of the voyage, too. A writer's life is a
very untrammeled and free life, and if there are hardships, there is some comfort in the fact we are not alone
with them, and never will be as long as the human race
continues. Economics are usually a problem, and
writers are always preoccupied with it, but this is part
of the game. And the game has its rules: the majority of
writers and artists must hold two jobs in their youth, a
job to earn money and the job of doing their own work.
It is a bit worse than that. The Authors League reports
that 95% of writers in America must hold another job
all their lives to make ends meet. If nature has not given
this extra strength, the love of writing and the need of
writing will give it. Like boxers, we may start to flag
after thirty, that is, not be able to do on four hours'
sleep any longer, and then we begin to curse government taxes and to feel that the aim of society is to put
us all out of business. It is then good to remember that
artists have existed and persisted, like the snail and the
coelacanth and other more or less unchanging forms of
organic life, since long before governments were
dreamed of.